Handbook of Environmental Disaster and Management

Attention Authors

'We Convert Fighters into Writers.' That's the motto of Manas Publications since more than four decades. Our message to the world is that India can win the battle not only by the bullet but also by the pen. There is no dearth of intellectuals in our country, but their knowledge is confined to them only. No sincere effort has been made by any other publisher to channelise their knowledge in national interest. That is why the talent of a large number of intellectuals remains latent. An author transforms his knowledge into a manuscript, and it is our job to spread his/her knowledge by converting it into a beautiful book. For over four decades, Manas has been motivating the intellectuals by publishing their manuscripts and would like to publish your manuscript too. So if you or your colleagues have any manuscript ready for publication or are working on it, kindly contact us with detailed synopsis and list of contents. We will transform your work into a valuable publication. If you wish, we can also suggest you the suitable subjects for writing the books related to your area of expertise. Manas is known for its publishing quality and commitments. We take utmost care in production and give wide publicity to the book as well as its author through our national and international distribution network.

Handbook of Environmental Disaster and Management

Thakur Shailendra Nath

Manas Publications
(We Convert Fighters into Writers)
New Delhi-110002 (INDIA)

MANAS PUBLICATIONS

(We Convert Fighters into Writers)

(Publishers, Library Suppliers, Importers & Exporters)

4402/5-A, Ansari Road (Opp. HDFC Bank)

Darya Ganj, New Delhi-110 002 (India)

Off. (23260783, 23265523, Fax: 011-23272766

E-mail: manaspublications@vsnl.com

manaspublications@gmail.com

ISBN 978-81-7049-435-5

₹ 695/-

Designed at

Manas Publications

Printed in India at

HS Offsets, Delhi

and published by Mrs Suman Lata for

Manas Publications, 4402/5-A,

Ansari Road, (Opp. HDFC Bank),

Darya Ganj, New Delhi-110 002 (INDIA)

Contents

Preface

It gives me immense pleasure to present my second book on environment, "Handbook of Environmental Disaster and Management" to the readers. It may be considered my small contribution for saving the environment. Though it is very difficult to capture the nature's terror in a small book, yet I have tried my best to group the famous global environmental disasters in the book's 12 chapters. Among these disasters are some of the deadliest earthquakes, terrorising tsunamis, disastrous tornadoes, blazing fires, nuclear radiations and oil spills. In spite of all his might, man is yet to conquer nature. Through effective and planned management, environmental disasters can be managed in a better way. It is a fact that in times of disasters, even one's enemy comes to help to mitigate one's suffering. This is human nature. And, after every disaster, man makes his surroundings better by new constructions. This happened in case of famous fire of London. After the fire, London was beautifully planned and rehabilitated. Even in India, Bhuj (Gujarat) after witnessing massive destruction and loss of life in the 2001 earthquake, now has been transformed into a place worth seeing.

The enormous devastation by nature makes people's condition pitiable. But they can brave devastation through stoicism. In the face of any nature calamity, the human spirit must remain strong despite uncertainty, hunger and hardships. These days most of the nations are either attacked by the malicious human agencies or are under siege by nature. In case of former it could be considered for punishment politically or through military stratagems but in latter case there is no deal to be struck with restless earth and rolling water. In this case necessity should appear to be the mother not of inventions, but prodigious patience. The philosophy of staunch detachment should be believed, neither to evoke pity nor invoke suffering. Be apathetic to the constant transmission of their contemporary pain. All sufferings are rooted in desire and indifference to passion is liberation.

I am obliged and indebted to my department and senior officers and colleagues who have provided necessary help and guidance in writing this book. The help extended by M/S Gupta Services, Gwalior, in typing of this book cannot be forgotten.

I owe a deep debt to my family members for their reverential and encouraging attitude. I would not have found a congenial environment at home for undertaking the onerous task of writing a book in difficult times, covering a wide range of complex issues of Environment.

I shall welcome criticism and suggestions for improving the quality of this book from the readers.

Thakur Shailendra Nath

Chapter – 1

Introduction

There are two big forces at work, external and internal. We have very little control over external forces such as tornadoes, earthquakes, floods, disasters, illness and pain. We have to make ourselves internally strong to boldly face the devastations caused by these disasters. Most of us have thought about how to prepare for storms. But there is another, even more important preparation we must make for tests that we are all certain to face. What we will need on the day of our testing is our spiritual preparation. After three years even a disaster can be good for something. The XIV Dalai Lama has said, "Tragedy should be utilised as a source of strength." No matter how enormous are our difficulties, how painful is our experience, if we lose our hope that is our real disaster.

According to the *Atharvaveda* "Prayer has been made to Mother Earth that she blesses us with the knowledge required to enjoy the treasures of nature but without disturbing the environmental balance." Entering the forest, He moves not the grass. Entering the water, He makes not a ripple. Trees are happy for no reason; they are not going to become prime ministers or presidents, and they are not going to become rich, and they will never have any bank balance. Look at the flowers — for no reason. It is simply unbelievable how happy flowers are. A human being is a part of the whole called by us as universe... Let's free ourselves from this prison by widening our circle of compassion to embrace all living creatures and the whole of nature in its beauty.

Earth is crammed with heaven. Sadly, though, earning a living, raising families and achieving success, most of us hardly take notice of this. It takes poets, or those with poetic ears, eyes and tongues to reconnect us to this state of noticing.

"Crammed with heaven" is that just right phrase from poet Elizabeth Barrett Browning: "Earth's crammed with heaven, And every common bush afire with God; But only he who sees, takes off his shoes..."

Once we learn to see with the eyes of the heart, or what Islamic mystics have called ***chasm-e-dil***, we begin to inhabit a world transformed by our seeing. The bland or unattractive reveals hidden beauty, the ordinary becomes sacred, everyday events take on a new meaning and depth. This living can be heaven or hell, depending on the perspectives that guide the choices that we make for ourselves and others, every single day of our lives.

Environmental Refugee

An environmental refugee is a person who can no longer gain a secure livelihood in his homeland because of drought, soil erosion, desertification, deforestation and other environmental problems, together with associated problems of population pressures and profound poverty. In their desperation, environmental refugees feel they have no alternative but to seek sanctuary elsewhere, howsoever hazardous the attempt. Not all of them have fled their countries, many being internally displaced. But all have abandoned their homelands on a semi-permanent, if not permanent, basis, with little hope of return.

It is profoundly disturbing that millions of innocent people in villages who live in perfect harmony with nature and rely on nature's bounties for their existence and survival, have to suffer for no fault of theirs. The world over, it is the poorest of the poor living around forest areas who defend the biodiversity, as they are dependent for survival on these resources. They have shielded thickly forested areas from being converted into wastelands. The forest and the vegetation that they preserve act as fresh water reservoirs that feed the rivers that quench our thirst and also irrigate our lands. It is solely because of villagers that the ecological balance remains intact. However, the village folks are more vulnerable to climate change including long spells of droughts and prolonged floods, unprecedented intensity of typhoons and cyclones, worsening food and water insecurity, increasing water–borne diseases, pest invasion, and destruction of traditional cultures linked with nature. In the face of increasing environmental disasters, we all need to do our bit to save the planet earth, rivers and all natural resources. If we continue to exploit our resources at the same pace then we will not be left with anything in the future. We will have to realise that if we destroy the environment, we destroy ourselves. Thus we are required to be more sensitive towards the environmental issues, their consequences and the natural resources that are available to us. We have to initiate positive actions and get the citizenry involved at each level. We should figure out ways wherein we can use our natural resources minimally.

Everyone must have seen the picture of Moshe, the small Jewish boy orphaned by the horrific 26/11 Mumbai terror attack, holding a ball in his hand. The boy indicates the possibility of using universe, being round in shape like ball, as healing tool, an emotional balm. Children can suffer different kinds of trauma. It can be as grave as being orphaned due to war, as is the case with the children in Afghanistan, or the trauma of children suffering from

HIV-AIDS in Africa or children who were orphaned during the Asian Tsunami of 2004. We need to understand that such disasters may shape a different type of future for the society.

It is reported that the Arctic melt may speed up climate change in twenty years. Scientists believe that the Arctic melt has potentially catastrophic implications. It could lead to an irreversible climate 'tipping point' within the next 20 years as a result of the release of huge quantities of organic carbon locked away as frozen plant matter in the vast permafrost region of the Arctic The signs of the Arctic melt are visible in the thawing out of billions of tonnes of frozen leaves and roots have lain undisturbed for thousands of years in the vast Arctic permafrost region of the northern hemisphere. Thawing of the Arctic permafrost region could release huge quantities of organic carbon locked away as frozen plant matter. A study into the speed at which the permafrost is melting suggests that the tipping point will occur between 2020 and 2030 and will mark the point at which the Arctic will turn from being a net 'sink' for carbon dioxide into a powerful source that will accelerate global warming. The study also found that by 2200 about two-thirds of the earth's permafrost will have melted, releasing an estimated 190 billion tonnes of carbon dioxide and methane into the air. "Our results show that as the Arctic warms up, frozen carbon will thaw out, releasing carbon into the atmosphere," said Kevin Schaefer of the US National Snow and Ice Data Centre.

Worldwide, carbon emissions are at their highest ever levels, stoking fears of a global temperature rise over the 'dangerous' 2° Celsius threshold, the International Energy Agency (IEA) announced. The world economy's return to growth in 2010 coincided with a 1.6 giga tonne rise in carbon dioxide emissions, the highest ever recorded jump, the agency said. "This significant increase in CO_2 emissions and the locking in of future emissions due to infrastructure investments represent a serious setback to our hopes of limiting the global rise in temperature to no more than two degrees," said IEA chief economist Fatih Birol. "Our latest estimates are another wake-up call," Birol said. "The world has edged incredibly close to the level of emissions that should not be reached until 2020 if the two degrees target is to be attained," he added. Scientists believe that a temperature rise of more than 2° Celsius would represent 'dangerous climate change'. The latest figures estimate that 30.6 giga tonne of carbon dioxide was emitted in 2010, a 5% jump from the previous record year, 2008.

Philosophy of Disaster

A disaster makes it painfully clear how fragile and mortal everything is. My parents, my son, my brother and sister, my friends and my beloved – all are in danger. It is so hard for me to conceive that there is nothing but the moment. The hard times of disaster make you aware of the reality as it is. It is always fragile; everybody is always in danger. Just that in ordinary times you are fast asleep, so you don't see the danger; you go on dreaming, imagining beautiful things for the coming days, for the future. But in the moments when danger is imminent then suddenly you realise that there may be no future, no tomorrow, and the present moment is what you have got. So the times of disaster are very revealing. They do not bring anything new into the world; they simply make you aware of the world as it is – they wake you up. If you don't understand this, you can go mad; if you understand this, you can become awakened. It depends on you how you use the moment: you can panic, you can go mad, you can break down in fear and start crying. But that is not going to help your family or your friends or your beloved. It is not going to help you either. The disaster has simply created a situation in which those who have a little intelligence can start devoting more and more of their time to meditation because tomorrow is really uncertain. It has always been uncertain, but now it is more uncertain than ever before. This disaster may be just the beginning of a chain of disasters. If anything goes wrong and now they know that one thing has gone wrong, then they do not have any power, they are simply helpless. They cannot control the energy that they are creating. The same disaster can happen in America, it can happen in Germany. Just next to this nuclear plant which has burned down and caused the disaster, there are two other plants of the same age; they were made at the same time and had the same architect. They must have the same faults. There is every possibility that the second plant will blow up soon, and the third will not be far behind. And, these disasters can trigger panic in thousands of people who are working in other plants. They can start committing mistakes that they have never committed just out of a feverish, frenzied state. And, it is only a question of pushing a wrong button. But you can use the disaster at the first plant as a great moment of learning to stay calm and composed in the face of extreme danger.

We are all always in danger. You know the old saying: "Never send to ask for whom the bell tolls. It always tolls for thee." When somebody dies, the church bell informs the whole village. But never send anybody to ask for whom the bell tolls, it always tolls for thee. Whoever may have died right now, each death is your death, because each death is a reminder that you are not going to be here forever. Each death is an opportunity to be awake. Before death comes, use the opportunity of life to attain something which is beyond death. It is pointless to be worried because you will be simply missing this moment of awakening, and you won't help anybody. And, it is not that only your parents and your friends, your beloved are in danger. In fact, the whole world is in danger. It is only a question of time. Somebody is in danger today, somebody else will be in danger tomorrow. But the danger is there for real. So, learn the secret of how to transcend the danger.

The secret is – start living more fully, more totally. Be more alert so that you can find within yourself something that is unreachable by death. That is the only shelter, the only security, the only safety. And, if you want to help your friends and family, let them become aware of this secret. What has happened is going to happen again and again because there are so many nuclear plants, even in undeveloped countries which do not have the technical knowhow. There are going to be disasters. This is just the beginning. Use the opportunity to be awake – that is all you can do. There is nothing else that you can do. So, use the moment for meditation because the disaster that has happened is not something that is finished once and for all. Its effects will linger for decades.

We are shocked when any earthquake and tsunami occurs. We are shocked by the unprecedented devastation. Our heart goes out to those who have lost their near and dear ones in this catastrophe. How can we help those who are suffering? More importantly, what can we do to restore the balance of nature and rhythm of Mother Earth? Energy in her destructive form is scary, but the same energy is so full of compassion in her manifestation of love. Let us join hands in praying to the Divine Mother so that she manifests her compassionate form to her erring children. Who else but a mother can forgive her children for their mistakes. Feel the pain of those who are suffering. Imagine as if it is happening to you or your dear ones and then open your heart out in fervent prayer to the Lord of the Universe, the Sustainer of life in this planet. Urge Him to have compassion for the afflicted. Pray with tears of devotion to melt the heart of the Most Compassionate One. Pray, meditate and evoke all the positive light in this world; that is the need of the hour.

Not even a leaf moves without the will of the Almighty. Everything that you do is not done by you. Deeds are done, events happen, but there is no individual doer. When you do something, who is the doer? I am sure you will say 'I'. And who is this 'I' you are referring to? Is this 'I' your body, your mind, or your intelligence? The next question is: Who runs the trillions of cells of your body in perfect harmony and coordination? Who runs this most unique instrument in the world? Your childhood is no longer with you; it is dead. Your adolescence is no longer with you; it is dead. If you have crossed your youth then your youth, too, is dead. But you are still alive! Did you ever ask who is this witness? Who has seen so many deaths in this short life span in the same body yet remains immortal? When you find experiential and intuitive answers to these few questions, you will get to know all about *karma* and its true doer.

Empathetic View of Life

Running through 'casualty' lists of those declared dead, injured or missing following an earthquake or a tsunami that hit the hardest, one finds the glaring lack of information on the corresponding damage to other life forms.

As an ecologist put it, the pressure and force caused by tsunamis and earthquakes could destroy coral reefs, fish populations, mangroves and other aquatic life. So natural disasters could be devastating not just for people. Moreover, what happens to the biosphere ought to concern us because as human beings we are not divorced from the ecosystems in which we live. Interestingly, ecosystems survive pretty well without humans but no human can survive without an ecosystem to cater to his/her needs.

If all things in the universe are expressions of a universal consciousness, it underlines the need for an empathetic perception – that is, to feel connected with other life forms besides fellow humans. If you do not have it in you naturally then you can cultivate empathetic perception by 'getting into the skin' of other life forms so that your world view is not exclusively anthropomorphic. Writing in the *Huffington Post*, Jeremy Rifkin says there is a strong connect between the growth of communication systems and expansion of human consciousness, and he makes the case for an empathetic civilization. We need to rethink human nature, he says, in what he calls the biosphere era. He votes for biosphere awareness and urges us to say goodbye to geopolitics.

Enlightenment thinkers like John Locke and Adam Smith subscribed to the thinking that the essential nature of human beings is rational, detached, autonomous, acquisitive and utilitarian. For them, individual salvation lies in unlimited material progress. These notions were reflected in the construct of nation states designed to protect private property and stimulate market forces while taking care of the collective self-interest of the citizens of a nation state in the global arena. The aim? Material gain. Things are not too different today, as political, administrative and geographical constructs are still designed to put the nation and citizenry above the self and consciousness.

Is this why we are unable to put in place a universal template for sustainable development that would include consciousness evolution? There is still hope, it seems, as growing scientific evidence shows that human beings are basically an empathetic species. This should help us realise our full potential as a species that is connected to all life forms.

The printed word helped organise the industrial revolution, created material prosperity and brought in ideological consciousness, says Rifkin. "Each more sophisticated communication revolution brings together more diverse people in more expansive and varied social networks... extending the range and depth of human social interaction." Rifkin says e-communication provides an ever more inclusive playing field for empathy to mature and consciousness to expand.

With renewable energy prospects and communication converging, our empathetic sensibilities could extend more spontaneously and symbiotically to the entire biosphere. According to Rifkin, just as habitats function within ecosystems and ecosystems within the biosphere in a web of interrelationships, governing institutions will function in a collaborative network of relationships across the globe (and perhaps beyond) as a whole. The synergy will ensure we are no longer anthropomorphic.

Environmental Disaster

An environmental disaster is a disaster to the natural environment due to human activity. The impact of alteration of the ecosystem by humans has led to widespread and long-lasting adverse consequences. This has resulted in death of humans, animals and plants and disrupted the human life leading to migration. Environmental disasters can have an effect on agriculture, biodiversity, economy and human health. The causes include pollution, depletion of natural resources, industrial activity or agriculture.

In the unforeseen consequences of manmade disasters and the results of war, one has remained and will remain constant—that is, the earth will be here long after man. Even the consequences of the worst environmental disasters can have an upside – the removal of humans from an area. If the apparent benefit is not immediately seen, the damage can be corrected through time. With the average lifespan of a human being at 78 years, the time will come when humans will be gone, and in just a few hundred years after their demise, the most prominent scars of our existence would heal and be forgotten. The one thing that the Earth will always have over humankind is time.

Natural disasters are often frightening and difficult for us to understand because we have no control over when and where they happen. What we can control is how prepared we are as communities and governments to deal with the dangers that natural disasters bring.

Places that are more likely to have natural disasters, such as the earthquake-prone Pacific Ring of Fire, or coastal areas vulnerable to hurricanes, require accurate methods of predicting disasters and warning the public quickly. Once the people have been informed, evacuation routes must be provided so that they can all leave quickly and safely, even if they travel by foot. Emergency warnings and evacuation plans are not enough, though. Where there is a high risk of earthquakes, buildings need to be strong and flexible enough to survive a quake without collapsing. Where hurricanes and flooding are a problem, levees and dams must be strong enough to hold floodwaters, and natural drainage systems must be maintained to allow waters to flow back into the ocean. The failure of the levee and drainage systems was responsible for most of the destruction and flooding in New Orleans after Hurricane Katrina in 2005. It was the poor planning of evacuation routes and assistance for those trapped by the flooding that resulted in many tragic fatalities.

People need to be educated on the risks in their area, and what to do when a disaster strikes. After a disaster, even if no one has died, there is a lot of damage to people's homes, farms and workplaces that must be repaired. This takes a lot of time and money to fix, and a country damaged by a disaster usually needs a large amount of international help to get better. Donated food, clothing, medicine and experienced professionals are all important when there is a disaster, but when the emergency is over it can take years to rebuild and make sure that future disasters can be managed. The Boxing Day tsunami which devastated Indonesia and the 2005 earthquake in Pakistan-occupied Kashmir were both natural disasters whose effects were made worse by underdeveloped infrastructure and widespread poverty. Tsunamis, earthquakes, hurricanes or any other natural disaster cannot be avoided, but with good preparation and well-organized help, it is possible to survive and go back to normal life after the disaster.

Following is list of specific events caused by the human activity that adversely affected the environment.

Agriculture

- Salinity in Australia
- Salinization of the Fertile Crescent
- The Dust Bowl in Canada and the United States (1934-1939)
- The Great Sparrow Campaign – Sparrows were eliminated from Chinese farms, which caused locusts to swarm the farms and contributed to a famine which killed 38 million people.
- Africanized bees, known colloquially as "killer bees"
- Mismanagement of the Aral Sea
- 'Dirty dairying' in New Zealand
- Hedgerow removal in the United Kingdom

Biodiversity

- Chestnut blight
- Extinction of American megafauna
- Extinction of Australian megafauna
- Deforestation of Easter Island
- Destruction of the old growth forests
- Rabbits in Australia
- Red imported fire ants
- Dutch Elm Disease
- Reduction in the number of the American bison
- Introduction of the Nile perch into Lake Victoria in Africa, decimating indigenous fish species

- The Saemangeum Seawall
- Emerald Ash Borer
- Environmental threats to the Great Barrier Reef
- 2006 Zakouma elephant slaughter
- Invasive species in New Zealand
- The loss of biodiversity of New Zealand
- Ghost nets
- Grounding of SS Makambo on Lord Howe Island
- Shark finning
- Decline of vultures in India due to Diclofenac leading to increased incidence of rabies

Coal

- Martin county sludge spill
- Tennessee coal sludge spill
- Mountaintop removal mining

Human Health

- Introduction of the Bubonic Plague (the Plague of Justinian) in Europe from Africa in the 7th century resulting in the death of up to 60% (100 million) of the population.
- Introduction of the Bubonic Plague (the Black Death) in Europe from Central Asia in the 14th century resulting in the death of up to 60% (200 million) of the population. The plague kept recurring until the 18th century.
- Introduction of infectious diseases by Europeans causing the death of indigenous people during European colonization of the Americas.
- Health effects arising from the 9/11 terror attacks
- The Goiania accident – human deaths resulting from dismantling a scrapped medical machine containing a source of radioactivity.

Industrial

- Minamata disease – mercury poisoning in Japan (1950s & 1960s)

- Ontario Minamata disease in Canada
- Itai-itai disease due to cadmium poisoning in Japan
- Love Canal toxic waste site
- Seveso disaster (1976) – A chemical plant explosion caused the highest known exposure of residential populations to 2,3,7,8- tetrachlorodibenzo-p-dioxin (TCDD). Bhopal disaster (December 3, 1984, India) – The leak of methyl isocyanate gas from the Union Carbide plant resulted in more than 22,000 deaths (and counting) and various genetic diseases that will continue to be seen for generations to come among the new-born. The disaster was caused by ignoring safety standards due to negligence and corruption by Warren Anderson, CEO of Union Carbide, a US company now a subsidiary of Dow Chemicals.
- Sandoz chemical spill into the Rhine river (1986)
- United States Environmental Protection Agency Superfund sites in the United States
- AZF explosion at a Toulouse chemical factory (2001)
- 2005 Jilin chemical plant explosions
- The Sydney Tar Ponds and Coke Ovens sites in the city of Sydney, Nova Scotia, Canada, known as the largest toxic waste site in North America
- Release of lead dust into Esperance Harbour
- Release of cyanide, heavy metals and acid into the Alamosa River, Colorado
- Summitville mine, causing the death of all marine life within a 17-mile radius
- Release of 20,000 gallons of lethal chemicals (metal sodium, trade name Vapam) into the Upper Sacramento River near Dunsmuir, causing the death of all marine life within a 38-mile radius.
- Release of CFCs resulting in ozone depletion
- Release of sulfur dioxide after a fire at the Al-Mishraq plant in Iraq
- The Phillips disaster
- Vila Parisi (Brazil)

- Health issues on the Aamjiwnaang First Nation due to chemical factories
- Environmental issues with the Three Gorges Dam
- Kingston Fossil Plant coal flyash slurry spill
- The Great Smog in London in 1952

Mining

Oil Industry

- Environmental issues in the Niger Delta relating to the oil industry
- Lago Agrio oil field issues
- Arctic Refuge drilling controversy
- Deepwater Horizon oil spill
- Sidoarjo mud flow triggered by Lapindo Brantas gas exploration in 2006, East Java, Indonesia

Nuclear

- Chernobyl disaster in 1986 in Chernobyl, Ukraine, killed at least 4056 people and damaged almost $7 billion of property. Radioactive fallout from the accident concentrated near Belarus, Ukraine and Russia and at least 350,000 people were forcibly resettled away from these areas. After the accident, traces of radioactive deposits unique to Chernobyl were found in nearly every country in the northern hemisphere.
- Mayak nuclear waste storage tank explosion (Chelyabinsk, Soviet Union, September 29, 1957) – over 200 people died and 270,000 people were exposed to dangerous radiation levels. Over thirty small communities had been removed from Soviet maps between 1958 and 1991.Windscale, United Kingdom, October 8, 1957–33 deaths reported after the fire ignited in plutonium piles destroyed surrounding dairy farms.
- Soviet submarine K-431 accident, August 10, 1985 (10 people died and 49 suffered radiation injuries)

- Soviet submarine K-19 accident, July 4, 1961 (deaths and more than 30 people were over-exposed to radiation)
- Nuclear testing at Moruroa and Fangataufa in the Pacific Ocean
- Fallout from the Castle Bravo nuclear test at Bikini Atoll in the Marshall Islands
- The health of Downwinders

Air/land/water

- Proliferation of plastic shopping bags

Air

- The Donora Smog of 1948 in Donora, Pennsylvania in the United States
- The Great Smog of 1952, which killed 4,000 Londoners
- The 1983 Melbourne duststorm
- The 1997 Southeast Asian haze
- The 2005 Malaysian haze
- The 2006 Southeast Asian haze
- Yokkaichi asthma in Japan
- Health problems due to the Jinkanpo Atsugi incinerator in Japan
- Kuwaiti oil fires

Land

- The Dust Bowl of Canada and the United States
- Contaminated soils in Mapua, New Zealand due to the operation of an agricultural chemicals factory
- Basin F, a disposal site in the United States for contaminated liquid wastes from the chemical manufacturing operations of the Army and its lessee Shell Chemical Company
- 2006 Cote d'Ivoire toxic waste dump

Water

Freshwater

- Sandoz chemical spill, severely polluting the Rhine in 1986
- Selenium poisoning of wildlife due to farm runoff used to create Kesterson National Wildlife Refuge, and the artificial wetland
- The Jiyeh Power Station oil spill in the Mediterranean region
- Effects of polluted water in the Berkeley Pit in the United States
- Ignition and conflagration (13 times from 1868 to 1969) of the Cuyahoga River in Ohio, United States
- Cheakamus River derailment which polluted a river with caustic soda
- Draining and development of the Everglades

Marine

- Coral bleaching
- The artificial Osborne Reef off the coast of Fort Lauderdale, Florida in the United States
- Dumping of conventional and chemical munitions in Beaufort's Dyke, a sea trench between Northern Ireland and Scotland
- Marine debris
- Environmental threats to the Great Barrier Reef
- Nurdles, plastic pellet typically under 5mm in diameter
- Friendly Floatees
- The Great Pacific Garbage Patch
- Minamata disease, mercury poisoning in Japan
- Mercury in fish
- Ocean acidification due to anthropogenic greenhouse gas emissions

Tragic Triumph

In a paradox that is both cruel and kind, destruction spurs reconstruction and acts as a stimulus for economic enterprise. Surveys have shown that, more often than not, stock markets which crash immediately in the wake of a catastrophe tend to gain new highs shortly after, as the work of rebuilding begins, generating large-scale production and employment. History reveals many such examples. The great fire which destroyed almost all of London in the 17th century – an eyewitness account of which is vividly presented in Samuel Pepys's famous diary – turned out in the long run to be more of a blessing than a bane. The conflagration scoured the city of the filthy, crowded hovels which were inevitable breeding places for plague-carrying rats and other disease-bearing vermin. Rebuilt, London came into its own as one of the biggest and richest cities in the world. The gilded monument in the City of London commemorates the Great Fire and its triumphant aftermath. Similarly, the great fire that engulfed Chicago in 1871 was seized by the 'City of Broad Shoulders', as poet Carl Sandberg would later describe it, as an opportunity to recreate itself in a new, innovative image. Their thriving city of cattle stockyards and grain silos reduced to smouldering ruins, Chicago's civic leaders invited architects from the world over to submit their most imaginative designs for its rebuilding. That is how what was billed as the world's first skyscraper – a 10-storey building – came up in Chicago, renowned today both for its robust local economy and the elegance of its architecture. (According to folklore the Chicago fire was caused by the twitching tail of a cow which knocked over an oil lantern and set ablaze a pile of hay.)

Japan itself, the only country in the world to have been the target of not one but two nuclear attacks, rose phoenix-like out of the ashes of a World War-II and went on to become a globally acclaimed 'economic miracle', the Land of the Rising Sony, a synonym for inventive industry. After the March 11, 2011 earthquake and the resultant tsunami that caused the accident at the Fukushima Daiichi nuclear power plant, Japan is once again a deeply wounded victim Will it once again overturn the disaster into remarkable victory? It can and it will, because it must. Not just for its own sake, but for the sake of that single fragile and yet indestructible bond that links humankind together – a bond and a lifeline called hope.

Japanese Prime Minister Naoto Kan described the catastrophic combination of earthquakes, tsunami and nuclear meltdown as the biggest crisis the country has had to face since the end of World War-II which was brought to an apocalyptic end with the atomic fireballs mushrooming over Hiroshima and Nagasaki. The bombs – codenamed Fat Boy and Thin Man – took a death toll of between 1,50,000 and 2,40,000 human lives. However, nature's fury in the form of the March 11, 2011 earthquake of Japan has claimed about 10,000 victims, showing that at its very worst, the destructive force of the natural world is far surpassed by the deadly ferocity of man's violence against man. The economic loss caused by the destruction of property and infrastructure cannot be calculated. In the midst of appalling devastation, it might seem like an obscene joke to suggest that a tragedy of this magnitude could possibly be turned eventually into a triumph. Yet curiously enough, time and again, not just the human spirit but also the laws of economics have proved amazingly resilient in the face of the most terrible of adversities, when widespread destruction has been taken as a challenge and an opportunity to rebuild with renewed enterprise and determination. The Gujarat earthquake of 2001 is an example. Surat, which was almost totally destroyed in the quake, sprang up out of the killer earth in a rejuvenated avatar, cleaner, better planned and more prosperous than ever before. Indeed, some might attribute the rise of Gujarat as an economic super-state to the seismic upheaval.

The mushroom cloud of nuclear catastrophe should not hang over any country even once. What *karma* is this deep and determined country, Japan, playing out? But, however unnerving the reality, equally stirring has been the 'super-human' effort to pull life out of the jaws of death. Once again there is manifest proof that feats can vanquish, delay and elevate defeat. We have watched this with as much awe as shock. A statesman-like government has not offered insultingly stupid reassurances, but has been as transparent as it can possibly be without swamping hope. A disciplined people have drawn on sustained disaster drills and, as much, on their cultural and spiritual wellsprings. All of us have wondered 'What if it were to happen here?' Official bumbling? Public panic? Yes. But we have enough devastation in recent times to show that we as individuals can be as brave, even superhuman. We may never have faced the challenge that confronted the band of workers who stayed on to calm Fukushima's furious core, or the 'kamikaze pilots' who remained undeterred by the slim chances of containment. We may never have faced an equal challenge, but through bomb blasts and deluge, we too have displayed the sacrifice of comparable value. We are our brother's keepers. And of other life too. The creatures swallowed whole by Japan's monster wave may be part of a cosmic cycle of destruction and creation.

Fukushima must not hamper India's nuclear energy plans

Equating Japan's Fukushima calamity to the 1986 Chernobyl (Ukraine) nuclear disaster by upgrading the former to level 7, the highest threat level in a nuclear crisis, should trigger a wholesale re-evaluation of how Indian reactors are planned and maintained. Even in risk-averse, industrially advanced Japan, a series of unwarranted events and human failure resulted in radiation leaks. Commendably the Fukushima reactor withstood a 9.2 magnitude earthquake just 130 km away, but the resulting tsunami was 2.5 metres higher than the reactor was planned to face and survive. This unimaginable barrage of water shorted the generators used to cool the reactor core. The final straw was callousness. The Tokyo Electric Power Company delayed cooling the core with seawater because it would irreparably damage the expensive equipment. If anything, this chain of events demonstrates why we must plan on the basis of Murphy's law that states if things can go wrong they will, and simultaneously. Contingency planning would benefit from informed public scrutiny of what is currently a closed governmental loop. A start would be reassessing the risk for reactors, but there is not any reason why every step of reactor design and building should not be made transparent.

India is the fifth largest producer of electricity in the world after China, the US, Japan and Russia. However, in per capita terms, it ranks around 150. China is at the 80th rank, Russia 26th, Japan 19th and the US 11th. Annual per capita electricity consumption, a key index of development, is at around 650-700 kWh in India. This is less than half of the average in non-OECD countries, one-fourth of the world average and 14 times less than the average in OECD countries. We need to decide what our target should be. In my view, 5,000 kWh appears a reasonable target. This is significantly better than the world average and about half the average in OECD countries. At this level of per capita electricity consumption for a projected stabilised population in India of around 1.6 billion, we need to add to Indian grids electricity generation of around 40% of the present-day global output. To realise the same target, China needs only about half as much. Our coal reserves can support electricity supply at such a level for around 11 years. Our total hydro electricity potential can provide for around 5% of the needed generation capacity. Other renewables excluding solar can support around 2%. Nuclear and solar energy are thus the only energy sources that can meet the challenge of our development. This does not mean less emphasis on other forms of energy generation. We need to make full use of all energy resources available to us.

We would need to earmark around 4.5 million hectares of area to be able to collect enough solar energy to meet our needs. This is roughly a fourth of the barren uncultivable land available in India. We, however, need aggressive development of this technology to make it cost-competitive. Also, since the sun does not shine on a 24 7 basis, we need cost-competitive energy storage technologies. There are other areas of development of energy technologies for the future such as fusion energy. We may well be at the oil peak around now. Our coal is likely to run out in around 40-50 years. Alternative energy supplies at the requisite level of use would need to be ready before this time. A severe energy crisis is likely to hit us much earlier than it does most of the world. We should look at nuclear energy in this backdrop. It already provides 16% of world electricity in a cost-competitive manner. Despite Fukushima or the earlier Chernobyl, TMI and other accidents, real risks with nuclear energy are the lowest compared to other energy forms used commercially. The advantage of nuclear energy would be even higher if one factors in the additional risks associated with the predicted consequences of climate change as a result of use of fossil fuels in a business-as-usual manner. Yet nuclear energy frightens us beyond all proportions. Fukushima so far has had no fatality caused by radiation. Seventeen workers have been exposed to doses in excess of 100 mSv, but that is lower than the permissible lifetime dose for occupational workers. There is radioactive contamination in the public domain, which will take quite some time to normalise. But the radiation dose received by people is unlikely to cause significant harm. The tsunami, which caused the accident at Fukushima, has taken more than 13,000 lives with more than 14,000 missing. Yet the Fukushima accident seems to occupy much larger media space. Seismically, the only region in India somewhat comparable to Japan is the Himalayan belt. As a matter of policy we do not locate a nuclear power station there. Epicentres that can potentially trigger a tsunami are around 10 times farther away in India's case as compared to Japan After the Fukushma accident, Japan has not shut down reactors that are operable. This is not to justify Fukushima. Such accidents are not acceptable. We must learn basic lessons from Fukushima and strengthen the safety of our nuclear activities without being complacent. We should also make rapid progress to bring in advanced reactor systems such as AHWR with their greater degree of inherent safety. However, the impending energy crisis, the risks of climate change and the limited time we have in tiding over these threats cannot be lost track of. The tendency to read catastrophe into anything nuclear and allowing panic to grip us and deprive India from fulfilling its aspirations would be a self-defeating exercise.

Politics should not hijack the nuclear debate. Several important concerns pertaining the use of nuclear energy need to be debated. However, the protests spearheaded against the proposed nuclear power plant in Jaitapur appear to ignore all of these for petty political ends. Such tactics merely divert attention from the real stakes: both India's energy future and our collective safety.

If the protesters were serious about fostering debate on the risks of nuclear energy, they would have adopted peaceful means to signal discontent. Instead, they chose violence, targeting a police station and a hospital, which suggests that their 'cause' has been hijacked by something other than the nuclear issue. If the protesters are misguided in their tactics, their call to cancel the Jaitapur project is an impractical knee-jerk reaction to Japan's Fukushima catastrophe. This suggests the need to educate the public about nuclear power, which will need to be part of India's energy mix. According to an expert, for India to become a developed country, power consumption has to increase by six to eight times. All of this cannot come from the polluting fossil fuels or renewables alone. Nonetheless, our nuclear establishment is in need of a dramatic overhaul. The nuclear watchdog, the Atomic Energy Regulatory Board, cannot continue as part of the organisation tasked with building plants, the Department of Atomic Energy. As for Jaitapur, its environmental clearances were granted within 80 days of the Nuclear Power Corporation of India submitting its impact assessment report. Now, the environment minister's call for 'deeper thinking' about Jaitapur begs the question what dynamics guide policy making vis-a-vis the complete life cycle of nuclear power plants. All of this remains cloaked in a web of secrecy.

India's Safety Record no Reason to be Complacent

There are raised voices against nuclear power both in civil society and among politicians around the world. In India, existing frictions over the proposed Jaitapur nuclear power plant have been exacerbated with opposition becoming more strident. Nuclear disarmament hawks have stepped in as well. But, as Prime Minister pointed out, India's safety record should be kept in mind as also the fact that the Kakrapar atomic power station withstood the Bhuj earthquake of 2002 while the Madras station came through the 2004 tsunami safely. It was shut down without any radiological consequences. Former chairman of the Atomic Energy Commission Anil Kakodkar too has vouched for the safety of our nuclear installations. Nor can we deny the necessity of nuclear power as part of a diversified energy basket, including renewable and conventional energy, for sustaining India's economic growth.

Like China, we have big plans on nuclear power, hoping to push up generation to 63,000 megawatts by 2032. It is therefore all the more necessary that we revisit safety issues. Safety measures at today's plants are constantly being upgraded, making them substantially safer than earlier installations. This should not make us complacent. Here and globally, there will be greater focus now on plugging every possible chink in safety assessments, and on choosing nuclear plant sites more carefully and strengthening the structural integrity of nuclear installations and reactor designs with better materials and technological inputs. This can only be good for the nuclear energy sector. The other positive is that countries are likely to focus more on renewables.

India must carry out a thorough safety audit of all its 20 nuclear power plants in the wake of the Fukushima disaster. We need data and expert reviews of the nuclear malfunction abroad and shore up safety features if required. But a summary conclusion about the viability and soundness of nuclear power would be wholly unwarranted. Specialists say that all our nuclear stations have been tested to withstand earthquakes and tsunamis. India's pressurised heavy water reactors have built-in features to keep the core cool even in a situation of plant blackout, with injection of fire water. And unlike Japan, the bulk of India's landmass is not as prone to seismic activity or tsunamis. However, India needs regular safety reassessment to manage risks better. India wants to generate 40,000 mw of nuclear energy by 2030, with modern nuclear technology. It should stay the course.

At a time when Disaster Risk Reduction (DRR) has become a key policy initiative worldwide for ensuring that there is a better preparedness in dealing with calamities, India is still seriously lagging behind. Nearly 100% of the funds meant for modernization of weather forecast, ocean movement and prediction of other natural disasters have remained unutilized. A Comptroller and Auditor General (CAG) report, tabled in the Parliament painted a grim picture of funds, which were to be used effectively for an upgraded weather forecasting system, lying idle. In the same way, finances allotted for better prediction of calamities such as earthquakes and tsunami and proper assessment of coastal erosion and landslides had not been used.

Between 2007-08 and 2009-10, almost the entire amount budgeted for modernization of the India Meteorological Department (IMD) and earthquake risk evaluation centre, development of seafront facility and desalination plant, aviation metrology and national centre for medium range weather forecasting had not been spent at all. Coming in the backdrop of Japan earthquake and tsunami disaster in which thousands perished and billions of dollars worth of infrastructure was destroyed, the CAG review reveals how the ministry of earth sciences reported savings of up to Rs 220 crore annually by the IMD. The startling aspect of this revelation is that the funds were meant for improvement of climate prediction, including monsoon. There was a proposal to divide the IMD modernization plan into various sub-projects such as Doppler Weather Radars, Automatic Rain Gauge Network and Automatic Weather System, etc. The savings occurred due to delayed approvals of the schemes, delays in procurement, construction and tendering and also slow initiation of the project activities, the CAG observed.

The National Centre for Medium Range Weather Forecasting was set up in Noida a few years ago to develop a global circulation model for preparing weather forecast up to three days in advance. A budgetary allocation of Rs 17 crore for this centre remained unutilized between the fiscals 2007 and 2010. It appears that no spending was possible because of the delayed approval for the installation of the supercomputers and for repairs at the centre. The major activity proposed for implementation during 2008-09 at this centre was to conduct assimilation experiments on satellite data using the super computer and thereby improve the operational weather forecast. A UN assessment has stated that half of the world's GDP is exposed to disaster risk. And it has also been said that countries "which have not invested in DRR are more likely to fail in achieving their full economic potential." The UN has already cautioned India to build capacity and work towards solutions to manage climate risks while investing at least 10% of all its rescue and rehabilitation funds towards disaster risk reduction.

Solar Activity and GCR Flux

A known cause of GCR flux changes is the change in solar activity of sunspots and solar wind. Variations in solar activity lead to changes in the solar magnetic field and the charged particle carrying solar wind extending into space. The more active the sun, the stronger the solar magnetic field and the solar wind. As GCRs diffuse into the centre of the solar system from outside, they get deflected and experience a reduction in their energy as well as intensity near the earth. That is, solar activity and GCR flux are anti-correlated. The reduced GCR flux will lead to a reduction in ionization, which, in turn, can lead to a decrease in the CC and the consequent increased warming of the planet.

Jan Veizer reported in 2005 a high degree of correlation between solar activity, GCR flux changes (as measured by the cosmic ray neutron monitor in Huancayo, Peru) and low-level CC changes (as derived from the infrared datasets of the ISCCP or the International Satellite Cloud Climatology Project). That is, besides the direct effect of solar irradiance on the earth, the sun can also have an indirect effect on the global temperature by modulating the GCR flux and CC formation near the earth. Reduction in CC results in reduced albedo radiation back into space, which causes increased warming of the atmosphere and increased global surface temperature. This, if true, implies that the effect of anthropogenic causes of global warming, like greenhouse gas (GHG) emissions, would be that much lesser if the GCR-induced cloud formation effects were properly taken into account. This is not to say that the Intergovernmental Panel on Climate Change (IPCC), which in its assessment report of 2007 (AR4) has held anthropogenic carbon emissions to be chiefly responsible for the observed global warming of 0. 75°C in the last 150 years since industrialization, has not taken cognizance of the possible impact of GCR on the global climate. This is what AR4 has to say on the issue "Various scenarios have been proposed whereby solar-induced GCR fluctuations might influence climate... Because of the difficulty in tracking the influence of one particular modification brought about by ins through the long chain of complex interacting processes, quantitative estimates of the GCR-induced changes in aerosol and cloud formation have not been reached." Specifically, with regard to the uncertainties in radiative forcing due to cosmic rays, it said, the evidence was insufficient, scientific consensus was low, the level of scientific understanding of the process was very low. And, while there was some empirical evidence as well as microphysical models that suggested a linkage to cloud formation, there was a general lack of understanding of the physical mechanism and there was uncertainty in correlation studies.

One reason why the effect of long-term changes in GCR intensity on the low-level CC and its impact on global warming were not clearly understood was the absence of reliable estimate of the GCR flux changes over a long period. This has now become available following the works of McCracken and associates who have estimated these flux changes through accurate proxy measurements of beryllium-10 (Be^{10}) obtained from the deep polar ice core. They have merged the long-term cosmogenic data of Be^{10} with actual GCR measurements from 1933 to 1965 and reconstructed the long-term changes in GCR intensity during 1428-2005. Further, McCracken and colleagues inverted this long-term cosmic ray data to yield the helio-magnetic field and observed a clear correlation with the observed sunspot data. The increase in the magnetic field so determined agreed with that directly measured by the Advanced Composition Explorer (ACE), the satellite mission of the National Aeronautics and Space Administration (NASA), launched in 1997.

In his commentary, atmospheric scientist V. Ramanathan makes the following observation: "The observed rapid warming trend during the last 40 years cannot be accounted for by the trends in GCRs. This does not by itself negate the importance of GCRs *as* a forcing factor of climate change, but strengthens the case for GHG forcing *as* the primary driver of climate change." Specifically, it is pointed out that while quantitative modelling studies do provide evidence for (a) ion production by GCRs and the formation of CCN, and (b) solar activity and increased CCN production and cloud drops at less than 3 km altitude, there are substantial differences and discrepancies in the various studies that attempt to establish the 'solar activity-CCN production-low clouds' link. "Given this...," he says, "we can neither categorically rule out a GCR-cloud connection nor conclude affirmatively about such a connection." Even if the satellite data were reliable, the correlation between the GCR flux changes and cloudiness may not be straightforward for the following reasons:

(a) While due to man-made emissions of aerosols, the abundance of CCN in all continental regions and oceanic regions is in the range of 1,000-5,000 particles/cm^3, cloud drop concentrations in most low-level clouds are less than 500 particles/ cm^3. In such heavily polluted regions, additional ionic sources from GCRs are not required to account for the observed cloud drop concentrations.

(b) Satellite cloud data began only in the 1980s. The large warming trends during this period would itself impact the cloudiness at regional and global scales. Thus analyses that attempt to attribute all cloudiness trends to GCRs may be misplaced.

(c) Observations of global average during the 20th century reveal three basic periods: warming trend during 1900-1940, slight cooling during 1940-1970, and the rapid warming trend that is continuing. However, the GCR trends underwent monotonic decrease from 1900 to 1970 and then levelled off. The trends do not seem to reflect the large warming trend during 1970-2010.

Molecular Clusters

On the basis of SKY results, Svensmark theorises the formation of CCN from molecular clusters *as* follows. Stripped by cosmic rays, electrons in the atmosphere attach themselves to fragile clusters of sulphuric acid and water molecules. Their electric charges stabilise the clusters while more molecules join them. When the molecular clusters are big enough, the electrons leave them in a stable state and catalyse other clusters to grow. In the previous theories of cluster growth, Svensmark points out, each electron was supposed to remain with just one cluster. "The catalytic behaviour of the electrons is much more efficient," he adds. This theory, he says, explains in detail the surprising quick production of droplets seen in the SKY experiment by his team. But it would seem that this picture does not quite match the cloud microphysics picture outlined by Gunturu. A more ambitious project called CLOUD (Cosmics Leaving Outdoor Droplets) at the European Organisation for Nuclear Research (CERN), has just begun to produce the first results that are yet to be published. The aim here, as in SKY, is to investigate the possible influence of cosmic rays on the earth's clouds and climate by studying the microphysical interactions involved. Whereas SKY used cosmic ray muons, CLOUD will use a beam from the high-energy particle accelerator. This is the first time that an accelerator is being used to study atmospheric and climate science. The initial stage of the experiment uses CERN's proton synchrotron to send a beam of particles into an ultra-clean reaction chamber filled with atmospheric gases. The effect of the beam on aerosol production will be recorded and analysed. The CLOUD project, after many hiccups, kicked off in 2006 and the experiment began in November 2009. This experiment should provide more detailed results on the GCR-cloud cover linkages and settle many of the outstanding questions. As of now, CLOUD has seen sulphuric acid and water combine to make particles when blasted by the CERN beam in a way that matches predictions of the most recent models.

Chapter – 2

Earthquake

Earthquake is a sudden movement of the earth's lithosphere, that is, its crust and upper mantle Earthquakes are caused by the release of built-up stress within rocks along geologic faults or by the movement of magma in volcanic areas. They are usually followed by aftershocks. Closer Look Fractures in the earth's crust, or *lithosphere,* where sections of rock have slipped past each other are called *faults.* Earthquakes are caused by the sudden release of accumulated strain along these faults, releasing energy in the form of low-frequency sound waves called *seismic waves.* Although thousands of earthquakes occur each year, most are too weak to be detected except by *seismographs,* instruments that detect and record vibrations and movements in the earth.

Primary and secondary waves radiate from an earthquake's focus and move through the earth's interior. As they encounter a boundary, like that between the lower mantle and the liquid outer core, they are reflected and refracted. Surface waves radiate out from an earthquake's focus and travel only along the earth's surface. The point where the earthquake originates is the seismic focus. Directly above the seismic focus on the earth's surface is the earthquake's epicenter. Three kinds of waves accompany earthquakes – primary (P), secondary (S) and surface (L) waves. Primary (P) waves have a push-pull type of vibration. Secondary (S) waves have a side-to-side type of vibration. Both P and S waves travel deep into the Earth, reflecting off the surfaces of its various layers. S waves cannot travel through the liquid outer core. Surface (L) waves—named after the nineteenth-century British mathematician A.E.H. Love—travel along the earth's surface, causing most of the damage of an earthquake. The total amount of energy released by an earthquake is measured on the Richter scale. Each unit (1) increase on the Richter scale corresponds to a ten-fold increase in the earthquake strength. Earthquakes above 7 on the Richter scale are considered severe.

Hawaii Earthquake History

Much of the early record of Hawaiian earthquakes comes from the diary of Mrs. Sarah J. Lyman, a missionary's wife. The Lyman family lived at Hilo, on the Big Island of Hawaii. Mrs. Lyman began her account in 1833 and continued it until her death in 1885. This record was then continued for eleven more years by her descendants. About four or five earthquakes per year were reported. On February 19, 1834, a strong shock threw down stone walls, stopped clocks, upset bottles, and sloshed milk out of half-full pans. Standing and walking were rendered difficult. A similar earthquake occurred on December 12, 1838. No volcanic activity was noted for either event. On March 27, 1868, whaling ships at Kawaihae on the west coast of Hawaii observed dense clouds of smoke rising from Mauna Loa's crater, Mokuaweoweo, to a height of several miles and reflecting the bright light from the lava pit. Slight shocks were felt at Kona on the west coast and Kau on the flanks of the volcano. On the 28 March, lava broke out on the southwest flank and created a 15-mile flow to the sea.

Over 300 strong shocks were felt at Kau and 50 to 60 were felt at Kona. At Kilauea the surface of the ground quivered for days with frequent vigorous shocks that caused lamps, crockery, and chairs to spin around as if animated. One shock resembled that of a cannon projectile striking the ground under the proprietor's bed, causing him to flee, according to the narrative published by C. H. Hitchcock in the *Bulletin of the Seismological Society of America* in 1912.

Between March 28 and April 11, 1868, over 2000 distinct shocks were felt at Kona. The main shocks struck on April 2, at 4:00 p.m., and again on April 4 at 12:30 a.m. A magnitude of 7 3/4 was estimated for this earthquake (by Augustine Furumoto in his February 1966 article on the Seismicity of Hawaii in the *Bulletin of the Seismological Society of America*) based on the extent of intensity reports. Instrumental recordings, the usual basis for computing magnitudes, were not available at this early date. The shock was felt throughout the islands as far as Niihau some 350 miles away. The ground rolled like a ship at sea and many walls tumbled down. A landslide three miles long and thirty feet thick swept down the hill carrying trees, animals, and men. Thirty-one people and thousands of cattle, sheep, horses, and goats were killed in the one slide. A seawave struck the coast from Hilo to South Cape, being most destructive at Keauhou, Puna, and Honuapo; 180 houses were washed away, and 62 lives were lost to the wave alone. A 10-foot-high wave carried wreckage inland 800 feet. Not a house survived at Honuapo. A stone church and other buildings were destroyed at Punaluu. Maximum wave heights were 65 feet, the highest observed on Hawaii to date.

An intense earthquake occurred on January 22, 1938, with a magnitude on 6-3/4 and a maximum intensity VIII on Mauna Loa. The epicentre, located under the ocean about 40 miles east of the island of Molokai, was about as far north as earthquakes occur in the Hawaiian chain. On Maui there was general panic with people rushing from theatres. Flashing lights were reported by many. Landslides blocked roads and cut water pipes. Several reservoirs and water tanks were damaged. A chimney fell and a transformer was thrown down at Hana. Windows were broken and walls were cracked at Kula. It was felt widely on the other islands with some damage on Molokai (pipes broken), Lanai (bottles thrown from shelves), Oahu (organ pipes out of sockets at Honolulu and the seismograph at the University was dismantled), and Hawaii (dishes broke, and some chandeliers fell). The earthquake was distinctly felt by two ships at sea.

A severe earthquake occurred on August 21, 1951, and had a maximum intensity of IX and a magnitude of 6.9. Scores of homes were wrecked or damaged on the Kona coast on the west side of Hawaii. Rocks fell from cliffs, causing a 12-foot wave. A landslide covered the famed Pali Kapu on Keoua burial grounds of Hawaiian royalty. Cracks six inches wide opened on the coastal highway. Walls of churches were thrown down in Hookena and houses moved from their foundations at Napoopoo and Kealakekua. Telephone service was out through most of the area. The collapsing of water tanks along the dry Kona coast led to a two-month dry season and made it necessary to truck water from Hilo.

In addition to the tectonic and volcanic local earthquakes, Hawaii is a frequent victim of tsunamis from distant earthquakes. The Catalogue of Tsunamis in the Hawaiian Islands by George Pararas-Carayannis lists 85 tsunamis since the earliest reported in 1813 or 1814. Of these tsunamis, 15 have caused significant damage. Only four of these, including the 1868 earthquake and tsunami described above, originated near Hawaii. Most were originated in the northwest Pacific and near South American coasts. In 1837 an earthquake in Chile sent waves 20 feet high against Hilo, Hawaii. Initially the sea receded and several were drowned by the returning wave while they were attempting to collect fish stranded on the exposed sea bottom. In all, 62 people were killed and over a hundred homes were destroyed. The most destructive tsunami in Hawaii occurred on April 1, 1946, following an Aleutian Islands earthquake. Waves 55 feet high, crest to trough, struck the northeast coast of Hawaii. At Hilo, 173 were killed, 163 injured, 488 buildings were demolished and 936 more were damaged. Damage was estimated at $25 million. The waterfront was washed out and breakwater and wharves badly damaged.

This tragic loss of life prompted the formation of the Tsunami Warning System so that Hawaii and the countries bordering the Pacific would never again be surprised by the large destructive waves.

Coping with Disaster Aftermath—Let's Learn from Japan

Powerful killer earthquakes have rocked one corner of the globe to another in just over a year between 2010 and 2011, but scientists warn against looking for a doomsday scenario in this recurring ripple of big earth-shaking natural disasters. "There's nothing going on out of the ordinary," Daniel McNamara, a research seismologist with the US Geological Survey, said. He said earthquakes happened 'all the time', with small tremors occurring in the tens of thousands each year.

The 8.9 magnitude Japan quake of March 11, 2011 struck after the January 2010 quake of 7.0 magnitude that devastated Haiti's capital and killed more than 300,000 people, followed by an 8.8 magnitude quake in April 2011 in Chile that killed more than 500 people. On February 22, 2011, a quake measuring 6.3 magnitude ravaged Christchurch, New Zealand.

"We've just had bad luck, they've occurred in places near to centres of population and then it becomes news," said Grenville Draper, professor of geosciences at the Earth and Environment Department of Florida International University. He and McNamara said it was human nature to try to assign patterns to events, including catastrophes.

Nature's Terror — Fire, Snow and Shaking Earth

Japan fought on March 13, 2011 to avert a meltdown at two earthquake-crippled nuclear reactors, describing the massive quake and tsunami, which may have killed more than 10,000 people, as the nation's biggest crisis since World War Two. The world's third largest economy was struggling to respond to a disaster of epic proportions, with more than 1 million without water or power and whole towns wiped off the map.

The nuclear accident, the worst since Chernobyl, sparked criticism that authorities were ill-prepared for such a massive quake and the threat that could pose to the country's nuclear power industry. Almost two million households were without power in the freezing north, the government said. There were about 1.4 million without running water. About 300,000 people were evacuated nationwide, many seeking refuge in shelters, wrapped in blankets, some clutching each other sobbing.

Bitterly cold and windy weather that was pushing into northern Japan was compounding the misery as the region struggled with shortages of food, fuel and water. Tokyo area residents began to buy and stockpile food, water, candles and batteries as shelves at grocery stores became increasingly bare. Prime Minister Naoto Kan went on national television to implore people not to panic. But there was plenty of panic in the stock market: Fevered selling drove down the Nikkei index by10.6% at the close of trading.

The initial wave scoured away entire communities, and desperate survivors searched for signs of friends and relatives who remained missing. There was plenty that was missing in the fishing village of Minamisanriku: the city hall, the hospital, the shipyard, police stations and 8,000 people. The tsunami might have crashed most heavily into this town that once was home to more than 17,000. Situated at the back of a mountainous V-shaped cove, the town was swamped by the first surge of muck and seawater that was 30 feet high as it roared between the valley walls.

Rescue teams from 13 countries pressed on with searches in other towns, some assisted by dogs. In the air, helicopters shuttled back and forth, part of a mobilization of some 100,000 troops, the largest since World War II.

Japan grappled with the aftermath of the terrible earthquake, the original gigantic one and its aftershocks, and a three-storey high tsunami. But, as pictures unfolded of buildings, ships, trains and hordes of cars being tossed and turned as so much flotsam and fiery jetsam on a swell of nature's fury, our rational selves bowed down in admiration for the systems and organisation in that country, which have successfully contained loss of human life to a few thousand. The tsunami toll in 2004, in contrast, had been 10,000 in India alone and overall 2,00,000, mostly in the developing countries that were ravaged then. This just goes to show the scope for planned, institutional preparation to minimise and mitigate the impact of natural calamities when they occur.

The Indian subcontinent is prone to dangerous earthquakes with five having taken place in the past two decades. The latest surveys indicate that about 60% of India's area is at some risk of experiencing an earthquake, and several major metropolitan centres including the national capital fall in high-risk zones. The World Health Organisation has rated India's disaster preparedness fairly well, but there is a difference between adequate policies and effective implementation. For instance, very few institutions here offer any training in earthquake engineering or integrate it with civil engineering. Even existing regulations are more honoured in the breach than in the observance. Disaster management is not integrated into developmental planning as is done in disaster-prone developed countries like Japan. Development of better building codes, strict enforcement of existing ones, creation of disaster management plans and response bodies from the local level to the central level, streamlining of the relevant administrative machinery with funding and jurisdiction clearly demarcated—these are all measures the government must take, and soon. Considering the possibility of a meltdown of nuclear reactors in view of the Fukushima disaster, a thorough safety audit of Indian nuclear plants must be conducted to test whether they can withstand the severest possible earthquakes.

Aftershocks Continue for Years

More than 100 aftershocks, with magnitudes ranging from 5 to 7.1, rocked Japan's east coast on March 12, 2011, a day after an 8.9 magnitude earthquake devastated the country, causing mass destruction. According to the US Geological Survey (USGS), 112 aftershocks of magnitude 4.0 or greater hit the same area as the original temblor and they continued with startling regularity. Eighteen of the aftershocks were of magnitude 6.0 or larger with one measuring 7.1. The aftershocks were in addition to 35 significant foreshocks over the week that preceded the massive quake of March 11, 2011. The most significant foreshock was a 7.2 magnitude temblor that occurred on March 9, 2011. According to experts aftershocks could go on 'for years', though they would get weaker with time. Dr Marcia McNutt, director of the United States Geological Survey, said the aftershocks are "the unnerving part of it (an earthquake)". "It's not just the five minutes of shaking from this earthquake, but it keeps going on and on and on, in terms of disrupting the lives of not only the citizens, but the relief workers too."

Japan Best-prepared Country Against Earthquake, Tsunami

Hidden inside the skeletons of high-rise towers, extra steel bracing, giant rubber pads and embedded hydraulic shock absorbers make modern Japanese buildings among the sturdiest in the world during a major earthquake. And all along the Japanese coast, tsunami warning signs, towering sea-walls and well-marked escape routes offer some protection from walls of water. These precautions, along with earthquake and tsunami drills that are routine for every Japanese citizen, show why Japan is the best-prepared country in the world for the twin disasters of earthquake and tsunami — practices that undoubtedly saved lives.

In Japan, where earthquakes are far more common than they are in any other country, the building codes have long been much more stringent on specific matters like how much a building may sway during a quake. Japan had clearly learned the lessons of the devastating Kobe earthquake of 1995, when it refused to accept offers of international help, leading to criticism that many of the 6,000 killed died unnecessarily. After the Kobe earthquake, Japan put enormous resources into new research on protecting structures, as well as retrofitting the country's older and more vulnerable structures. Japan has spent billions of dollars developing the most advanced technology against earthquakes and tsunamis. Japan has outfitted new buildings with advanced devices called base isolation pads and energy dissipation units to dampen the ground's shaking during an earthquake. The country that gave the world the word tsunami built concrete seawalls in many communities, some as high as 40 feet, which amounted to its first line of defence against the water. In some coastal towns, in the event of an earthquake, networks of sensors are set up to set off alarms in individual residences and automatically shut down floodgates to prevent waves from surging upriver. But Japan's "massive public education program" could in the end have saved the most lives, said Rich Eisner, a retired tsunami preparedness expert.

Japan mobilised 50,000 military and other rescue personnel on March 11, 2011 to spearhead a Herculean rescue and recovery effort, a day after being hit by its most devastating quake and tsunami on record. Every wing of the Self Defence Forces was thrown into frantic service, with hundreds of ships, aircraft and vehicles headed to the Pacific coast area. International search and rescue teams also rushed to the devastated country, some fresh from work in quake-hit New Zealand, including a 63-strong Japanese team that spent two weeks helping after the Christchurch quake. Emergency staff in Japan dug through rubble and plucked survivors off the roofs of submerged houses. The United States ordered a flotilla including two aircraft carriers to the region to provide aid. Army helicopters airlifted people off the roof of an elementary school in Watari and naval and coastguard choppers rescued 81 people from a ship that had been hurled out to sea.

The Indian rescue workers did a remarkably good job in comparison to the rescue workers of USA and military men of Japan. A Japanese official accompanying the Indian rescue workers stated that though the USA and Japanese rescue workers were doing their job with sensors and other modern equipments, the Indian workers simply used their hands. The Japanese villagers were impressed by their labour and diligence. The Indian workers searched and excavated dead bodies from places where all modern equipments and sensors used by others had failed miserably. The Japanese villagers were so impressed that they started saying "Dhaniyabad" instead of "Dhanyabad" for thanks at the time of their departure from Japan.

Earth's Axis Wobbles, islands Shift

The earthquake-cum-tsunami packed such fury that it has moved Japan's main island, Honshu, by about 8 feet. It has also caused the earth's axis to wobble by about 4 inches—something that experts say will lead to the shortening of the day by 1.6 microseconds, or just over a millionth of a second. These very tiny changes happen because of changes in the speed of rotation of the earth as surface mass gets shifted around in earthquakes. As portions of the earth's surface shift, there is a bit of an extra wobble in the planet's rotation around its axis. This causes an increase in the speed of spinning, resulting in shortening of the day. This, however, will have no impact on life on the earth. The 2004 Asian tsunami had clipped the earth's day by 6.8 microseconds and shifted its axis of rotation by about 3 inches. The Chilean quake of 2010 too shortened the day by 1.26 microseconds and changed the axis by 3 inches.

The shifting of islands was observed in the 2004 tsunami too. The topography or layout of the Andaman and Nicobar islands was palpably changed. The southern Nicobar group of islands saw permanent subsidence of about 15 feet while the northern Andaman Islands saw a lift of up to five feet. After the 2004 quake which caused the Asian tsunami that hit Indonesia the hardest, some of the smaller islands off the coast of Sumatra moved by a much as 20 metres and its northwestern tip shifted to the southwest by 36 metres. That temblor was considered more powerful than the recent Japanese one, measuring 9.1 in magnitude.

The Japanese quake caused a 400 km long and 160km-wide rupture in the earth's crust as one tectonic plate drove under another off the coast of northern Japan. This led to an upheaval in the sea above it, sending a 30-foot wall of water racing up to 10km inland in Japan and reaching California across the Pacific Ocean 10 hours later. Several small island states in the Pacific experienced 2-3 feet high waves, which were ripples of the Japanese tsunami as it went bouncing across the ocean.

Nuclear Bombs still Kill and Maim in Japan

In 1945 the world witnessed the first and hopefully the only use of the nuclear bomb in a war. The atom bombs killed about 90,000 to 166,000 people in Hiroshima and another 60,000 to 80,000 in Nagasaki. But apart from these people who sustained direct injuries from the bombs and died within four months of the incident; the exposure to radiation had a lasting effect on the survivors.

In the 1950 national census, 2.8 lakh people reported exposure to the radiation and to study the effects of radiation on human beings about 94,000 of these survivors were selected for a lifelong follow up. These people are under observation of the Radiation Effects Research Foundation (RERF), a cooperative US-Japan research foundation. To compare with the unexposed people another 27000 residents of Hiroshima and Nagasaki, who were not in the city at the time of bombing were also included in the follow-up program. It is now established that the most significant effect of radiation exposure is the increased risk of cancer. From 1958 to 1998 cancer other than leukemia was diagnosed in 7,851 of the 44,635 observed people. Apart from this 204 leukemia related deaths were also reported in another sample consisting about 49000 people. The extremely high rate of cancer is attributed to the radiation. Cancer is not the only disease triggered by radiation exposure as it is established that the survivors have also showed vulnerability to uterine myoma (non-cancerous tumor), chronic hepatitis and liver cirrhosis, thyroid disease, cardiovascular disease and cataract. It was found that there was a decline in the immune system of these people making them more vulnerable to general diseases as compared to those who were not exposed to radiation. The bomb had a horrific effect even on those who were exposed to radiation while they were still in their mother's womb. While these people are less vulnerable to cancer compared to the ones who suffered direct exposure, they have a higher incidence of mental disability. Contrary to the popular belief that the bomb will have genetic effect which will be passed onto the children of the survivors, no such incidents have been reported so far. But this might be because the past studies had limited ability in deciphering genetic mutation. May be in the coming years it will become clearer whether the effect of the bomb will go away with the last survivor or it will keep haunting the Japanese for generations.

Radioactive iodine in sea water off Fukushima

Radioactive iodine in seawater near an outlet at the Fukushima 1 nuclear power plant had been detected at 147 times the safety limit. It was earlier reported that radioactive iodine in sample water, taken at 100 metres from the shoreline in the vicinity of the nuclear reactors, was 29.8 times the permissible limits. The authorities began the daunting task of distributing bottled water to the families of an estimated 80,000 infants, defined as children under 1 year age. Authorities however said that iodine in the water had returned to safe levels. India had sent 10,000 litres of bottled water to Japan

Nuclear Renaissance Threatened after the Fukushima Explosion

Global expansion of nuclear power drew more scrutiny and skepticism as the world watched Japan struggle to prevent a meltdown at the Tokyo Electric Power Co's

Fukushima Daiichi No.1 reactor. The reactor was damaged by an earthquake of record intensity on March 11, 2011. Japan grappled to contain its worst nuclear accident in at least 33 years at the Fukushima plant north of Tokyo. Radiation levels around the Tokyo Electric Power Co station in Fukushima, 135 miles north of Tokyo, rose after cooling systems at a second reactor failed, heightening concerns about a possible meltdown. Water levels fell at a third reactor, raising the possibility of a hydrogen explosion there. But fortunately nothing more untoward happened after the March 11 explosion.

However, the March 11 explosion was itself enough to raise worldwide concerns about the safety of nuclear power plants. Peter Bradford, a former member of the US Nuclear Regulatory Commission, considered the Fukushima disaster "a significant setback for the so-called nuclear renaissance." He said, "The image of a nuclear power plant blowing up before your eyes on a television screen is a first... Those who advocate nuclear power, which emits virtually no carbon dioxide, as a way to combat climate change will now have to deal with a greatly heightened skepticism and heightened unwillingness to have nuclear power plants located in one's own neighbourhood.

There are 442 reactors world-wide that supply about 15% of the globe's electricity, according to the London-based World Nuclear Association (WNA). There are plans to build more than 155 additional reactors, most of them in Asia, and 65 reactors are currently under construction, the WNA said on its website. Japan gets about a third of its electricity from 54 nuclear power plants, the third largest consumption of nuclear power after the US and France. In Japan, two reactors are under construction and 12 more are planned, according to the WNA. China is tripling the number of its reactors, building 27 units to add to the 13 operating reactors on the mainland. In the

US, companies including Southern Co and NRG Energy have submitted applications to build as many as 21 new reactors, adding to 104 existing units.

Success in cooling N-reactors

Japan restored power to a nuclear reactor on 20th March 11 after 10 days in its race to avert disaster at a plant wrecked by an earthquake and tsunami that were estimated to have killed more than 15,000 people in one prefecture alone. Three hundred engineers had been struggling inside the danger zone to salvage the six-reactor Fukushima plant in the world's worst nuclear crisis since Chernobyl 25 years ago. The situation improved step by step. At the nuclear plant, workers braving high radiation levels in suits sealed in duct tape managed to connect power to the No 2 reactor, crucial to their attempts to cool it down and limit the leak of deadly radiation.

Officials at Tokyo Electric Power Company (TEPCO), which operates the plant, said the workers aimed to restore the control room function, lights and the cooling at the No 1 reactor, which was linked to the No 2 reactor by cable. Encouragingly for Japanese transfixed on work at the Fukushima complex, the most critical reactor—No 3, which contains highly toxic plutonium—stabilized after fire trucks doused it for hours with hundreds of tonnes of water. The water was having a cooling effect.

The Japanese art of stoic silence

The enormous earthquake and towering tsunami made Japan seem to pitiable but the really seismic aftershock of this story is the self-possessed stoicism of the Japanese people. On live television, on radio, in newspaper reportage and anecdotal accounts, their spirit appeared strong and unwavering despite nine days of unremitting uncertainty, hunger and hardship. The pronounced lack of self pity appeared to be at odds with a micro-chipped 21st century that transmits the merest pain round the world in microseconds. Contrast this Japanese reserve on display to a wondering world with America's righteous angst when the planes hit the Twin Towers and India's trembling-lip outrage after the Mumbai attacks. The US and India had, of course, been attacked by malicious human agencies; the Japanese were under siege by nature. The US and India could consider political and military stratagems to punish, perchance to prevail; for the Japanese, there was no deal to be struck with a restless earth and its rolling waters. In Japan, necessity appears to be the mother not of invention, but of a prodigious patience. Japan's bestselling author Haruki Murakami once described his countrymen's patience as "an attention to sound to silences." Might there be more to the Japanese stiff upper lip? How can a devastated country quietly go about its daily business obediently paying attention to "sound, to silences" over the great roar of the 21st century?

Tadao Ando, one of Japan's most famous architects, who forded the east-west divide to win the architecture Nobel, the Pritzker Prize, describes Japanese detachment as follows: "...the temple is made of wood. The divine spirit inside the building is eternal, so the enclosure doesn't have to be." It chimes with the early Stoics' argument "wherever I go it will be well with me, for it was well with me here, not on account of the place, but of my judgments which I shall carry away with me." Murakami's 2002 post-Kobe collection of stories, *After the Quake*, is about people suffering from what he calls the echo of the earthquake. Many of these characters might be in the eye of the world's cameras today. New footage offers glimpses of their self-contained universe and reveals that they can tell where awful truth and horrendous metaphor start to mingle. But actually this was a surprise to the Japanese themselves.

1993 Latur earthquake

The Latur earthquake struck India at 03:56 local time (UTC + 04:30) on September 30, 1993. The magnitude of the earthquake was 6.4 Mw and depth was 12 k.m. The main area affected was the Maharashtra State in western India. The earthquake primarily affected the districts of Latur and Osmanabad including Ausa block of Latur and Umerga of Osmanabd. A total 52 villages were demolished and about 30,000 people died and 30,000 were injured. It was an intraplate earthquake. The earthquake's relatively shallow focus of 12 km deep led shock waves to cause more damage.

The Latur earthquake proved enormously destructive because it occurred at 3:45 am when people who came in its ambit were indoors and asleep. The coordinates of the earthquake's epicentre were N18.07 and E76.62. This was very close to Latur which suffered the most damage. Killari, where the epicentre of the quake was believed to be located, had a large crater, which remains in place to date.

The Latur earthquake was one of a very rare type of earthquakes. It was what is referred to as a SCR (stable continental region) earthquake. An SCR earthquake occurs only about once per 100,000 years, making its predictability close to zero. According to scientists, it was not even possible for an earthquake to strike this region, There were not any monitoring stations in this region. Most earthquakes are a result of interaction between two plates, whether they be sliding, colliding, or forming a subduction zone. However, in this instance, the cause is very complicated. The Latur earthquake was an intraplate earthquake, or it occurred in the middle of a plate, as opposed to a plate boundary. The earthquake's epicentre was very far from any fault line. The cause of this earthquake is still in speculation.

The Latur earthquake was tremendously destructive. However, the earthquake itself did not cause as much damage. Most of the people were living in houses made of stones on soft soil. The tiles of the roofs were generally constructed out of stone plates, which were used as a result of availability and cost effectiveness. The tremors caused these plates to literally bury the local populace without food, water, and sometimes even air. The liquefaction, which resulted from the earthquake, destroyed the foundations of the houses and caused them to crumble. More than 60 percent of the deaths were a result of this. Liquefaction is the phenomenon that causes soft soil or sand to shake loose as a result of seismic activity.

There were several short-term and long-term effects of the Latur earthquake. The most tragic effect was that around 30,000 people died due to the primary and secondary hazards caused by the earthquake. The effects of this earthquake were accentuated, as the region had problems with structurally unsound buildings and the earthquake occurred at night while everyone was sleeping, giving the people less time to react. The hardest hit villages were those of the Latur and Osmanabad districts. The earthquake has left one good mark on India. In the aftermath of the earthquake, the Indian government diverted more funding into earthquake research. Also, more earthquake monitoring centres have now been made. Since, India is an LEDC, it has taken a much longer period of time for the region to recover completely from the catastrophe. In LEDCs, the recovery period is generally longer than in an MEDC. Also, the amount of deaths would have been lower as the engineering firms of an MEDC would have built the house foundations on bedrock, instead of having shallow foundations in soft soil. Finally, there would have been a host of building techniques in MEDC that would have cut the number of dead by two thirds, for example, the use of rubber shock absorbers and steel girders to prevent the snapping of columns and support structures.

Relief work during the primary stages involved rescuing people who had been trapped in the debris. Several foreign and local donors reacted immediately to the tragedy by sending relief teams and rescue workers. The first convoy of over 120 trucks laden with relief material such as tents, blankets, food and clothing, medical supplies and temporary shelters given by international donors departed from Mumbai on October 2, 1993. The Indian Army, State Reserve Police Force, Central Reserve Police Force and other law enforcement agencies had rushed their personnel almost immediately after the quake, assuming there would be a greater number of casualties.

Gujarat Earthquake of 2001

The 2001 Gujarat (Bhuj) earthquake occurred on January 26, 2001—India's 51st Republic Day—at 08:46 am local time (3: 16 UTC) and lasted for over two minutes. The epicentre was about 9 km south-southwest of the village of Chobari in Bhachau taluka of Kutch district of Gujarat. India. The earthquake reached a magnitude of between 7.6 and 7.7 on the moment magnitude scale and had a maximum felt intensity of X (Intense) on the Mercalli intensity scale. The quake killed around 20,000 people (including 18 in south-eastern Pakistan), injured another 167,000 and destroyed nearly 400,000 homes. The final death toll in Kutch was 12,220. Bhuj, situated only 20 kilometres (14 miles) from the epicentre, was devastated. The Mw 7.6 Bhuj earthquake was the most deadly in India's recorded history. One month after the earthquake, official Government of India figures placed the death toll at 19,727 and the number of injured at 166,000. About 600,000 people were left homeless, with 348,000 houses destroyed and an additional 844,000 damaged. The earthquake reportedly affected, directly or indirectly, 15.9 million people, nearly 50% of the population of Gujarat. More than 20,000 cattle were reported killed. The Government estimates placed direct economic losses at \$1.3 billion, although more recent estimates indicated losses of about \$5 billion. Considerable damage also occurred in Bhachau and Anjar with hundreds of villages flattened in the talukas of Anjar, Bhuj and Bhachau. Over a million structures were damaged or destroyed, including many historic buildings and tourist attractions. The quake destroyed around 90% of homes, eight schools, two hospitals and 4 km of road in Bhuj and partly destroyed the city's historic Swaminarayan temple.

In Ahmedabad, Gujarat's commercial capital with a population of 4.6 million, as many as 50 multi-storied buildings collapsed and several hundred people were killed. Total property damage was estimated at \$5.5 billion. The quake destroyed 80% of usable food and water supplies in Kutch. The district collector Anil Mukim oversaw the early delivery of aid and equipment to affected villages but later called for aid to cease as it encouraged a "relief mentality" which would delay a return to normal life. The four urban centres of Kutch, namely Anjar, Bhuj, Bhachau and Rapar were replanned after the earthquake. The Bhuj city which had an area of 19 square kilometre before the earthquake was expanded to an area of 56 square km. Three relocations sites were developed to decongest the inner city of Bhuj. The names of these sites are — Rawalwadi, RTO and Mundra site.

More than 100,000 fatalities from earthquakes have occurred on the Indian Plate in the past two centuries. Prior to 1800, the historical record is incomplete although we know of no event in the past millennium that has claimed as many lives as the Bhuj event (Bapat *et al* 1983; Iyengar and Sharma, 1998). The government estimates followings the Kangra, 1905 earthquake indicated 19,500 fatalities (Ambraseys & Bilham, 2000). The 1737 Calcutta cyclone is mistakenly included in many lists of Indian earthquakes (Bilham, 1994). The rate of occurrence of fatal earthquakes in the past two decades is more than double its mean value in the past two centuries.

The Bhuj earthquake occurred on the Kutch peninsula which has a long history of strong earthquakes. The region is bordered to the north and to the south by ancient rift systems. Structures within these rift systems and on the Kutch mainland are now subjected to compressional stress and reverse faulting resulting from India's collision with Asia. Compresssional features appear to be of at least two different ages, with folding events occurring prior to 120 Ka and a distinct set of new features activated much more recently.

The first historical Kutch earthquake to attract international attention was the 1819 Allah Bund (Dam-of-God) earthquake, which created a 6-m-high, 6-km-wide natural dam across the Puran or Nara river (which enters the Rann of Kutch from the north). A lake 30 km in diameter, Lake Sindri, was formed south of the Allah Bund and although this is now partly filled with sediments and evaporites, it remains as a monsoon-filled depression to this day. A lake also formed north of the Bund in 1819 which drained in 1826 when a torrent broke through several artificial dams on the Puran and cut a gorge through the Bund, flooding regions downstream. The geometry of this gorge was investigated briefly by Sir Alexander Burnes whose two accounts (in 1826 and 1827) differ in numerical detail. Captain William Baker, a canal engineer of considerable integrity, undertook a precise spirit levelling line across the Bund in 1844, but his important cross-section was mislaid in Bombay in 1846, and not discovered for more than a half century. From the details of Baker's levelling line, and the assumption that the measured topography is entirely due to the 1819 earthquake, it is possible to infer 11.5±1m of reverse slip on a NNE dipping fault that terminated 300-600 m below the surface.

Damage to Bhuj and Anjar during the 1819 earthquake was substantial. Much like those from the 2001 event. Damage reports from 1819 describe widespread collapse of structures on the Kutch mainland, accompanied by substantial liquefaction features in the Rann of Kutch. Damaging earthquakes also occurred in 1845, 1856, 1857, 1864, 1903, 1927, 1940, 1956 and 1970 in the Kutch region but with less severity (5<M<6). The most recent of these are well located and the others are known only by accounts of local damage. The events of 1845 were felt in Karachi and are reputed to have generated a tsunami and to have caused changes in channel depth near and north of Lakput on the western edge of the Kutch peninsula.

Events in 1856 and 1857 are known from reports in accounts of the Great Trigonometrical Survey of India. The 1956 Anjar earthquake killed 152 people. The mechanism of the 2001 Bhuj earthquake is currently unresolved, although, as in the 1819 and 1897 earthquakes, the event apparently occurred on a steeply-dipping thrust that did not break the surface. An unusual feature of the event is that aftershocks have occurred at considerable depth (20-30 km) suggesting rupture through much of the lithosphere. This appears to have similarities with the great 1897 Assam earthquake that occurred on a deep, steeply south-dipping reverse fault beneath the northern edge of the Shillong plateau. Aftershocks appear to favour a south- dipping rupture for the nodal plane of the 2001 main shock (Johnston, personal communication 2001). Slip appears to have been less in 2001 than in 1819, although it is possible that a careful examination of the recent earthquake will reveal new insights into the mechanism and magnitude of the 1819 event.

Seismic Productivity in Kutch

The Kutch region is more than 200 km from the closest plate boundary; hence the Bhuj earthquake occurred within the Indian Plate, albeit near a transform boundary. Geodetic measurements of plate deformation between southernmost India and the northern edge of the Gangetic Plain indicate a contraction rate of the Indian Plate of 3±2 mm/yr. Were this entirely concentrated in the Kutch region, it would result in a minimum recurrence interval of approximately 1000 years for earthquakes such as the ones in 1819 and 2001 (assuming a dip of 45°on the causative faults). Historic data record at least one severe earthquake in the region west of Kutch in about 1000 AD and perhaps another to the NE of the Allahabad in 1250-1300. Paleoseismic investigations of the 1819 Allah Bund revealed several pre-historic earthquakes in the past three millennia consistent with this view. However, since contractile strain almost certainly occurs elsewhere in India, it is possible that the deformation rate in western India is higher than in eastern and central India. Survey-mode GPS measurements that might confirm or refute this possibility were initiated in this region only in the past few years. The 188-year interval between the 1819 and 2001 events cannot be explained purely by a simple failure-strain replenishment process. We estimate approximately the dilatational strain fields that may have accompanied these events, calculated using boundary element methods. We approximate the Allah Bund rupture as a 90-km-long, 20-km-wide, planar dislocation with an average slip of 6 m with N 18° W strike. The geometry of the Allah Bund event is much simplified in this model since its relict surface expression is quite sinuous and possibly segmented. We apply a regional compressive strain to the Gujarat region to emulate the regional compressive stress azimuth characterised by recent seismicity and measured principal stress directions. The result of this model suggests that the earthquakes of 1845-1865 were partly in response to the westerly-directed lobe of compression from 1819, although this is clearly speculative given our poor understanding of the epicentral regions of these events. The Anjar 1956 and Bhuj 2001 earthquakes occurred in the easterly-directed lobe of increased compressive stress from the 1819 event. The region now inferred to be subject to enhanced strain contraction (compressive stress) has extended eastward, although its detailed geometry depends critically on the availability of the co-seismic deformation field which is currently ambiguous. We know of no specific earthquake in the Ahmedabad region in the historical record. However, a large tsunami is reported to have occurred in 1524 that caused considerable alarm to the Portuguese fleet assembled offshore at 17°34'. A violent earthquake occurred in southern Gujarat in 1705, and minor shaking is reported at Surat in 1663 and 1684.

Geodesy

The 2001 Bhuj earthquake occurred near the northern edge of a dense network of primary and secondary triangulation points of two first-order triangulation networks—the Kutch Coast Series and the Kathiawar Meridional Series. These triangulation networks form part of the Great Trigonometrical Survey of India (GTS) that was completed towards the end of the 19th century. The principal triangulation of the Kutch region was completed in May 1858 with a mean angle measurement accuracy of 7 μradians, with the exception of a small number of angles in western Kutch that included lines-of-sight that grazed hillsides (± 15 μrad). Anticipated co-seismic epicentral angular changes are expected to exceed 100 μradians. The original survey monuments consist of subsurface marks on bedrock, or on a buried stone tablets, surmounted by masonry columns with cemented upper marks. Each mark consists of a 1-cm-diameter chiselled depression surrounded by a 15 cm chiselled circle. The field teams discovered some of the points intact, but in many cases new points were established consisting of pins cemented into exposed rock outcrops.

Two moderate earthquakes occurred during the initial surveys. According to survey officer D. J. Nasmyth, the November 1856 earthquake distorted angles by up to 24 μrad in a triangle of the Kathiawar series approximately 25 km east of Bhachau. Two months later (in January 1857), an earthquake was sufficiently severe to damage the 4-m-high column at Khari Rohar 15 km ESE of Anjar (23°5' 70°13'), threatening to overturn the 18-inch theodolite upon it. A levelling network from Ahmedabad through Bhachau to Anjar included some of these triangulation points in 1874-5 and in 1889-90. When these heights were re-measured after the 1956 Anjar earthquake, it was discovered that elevation changes of up to a metre had occurred.

Despite, these indications of significant and repeated deformation, and despite important recent progress in implementing GPS geodesy in India, no GPS control specifically for earthquake-related studies had been established in the Kutch region prior to the earthquake. To our knowledge, no published record exists of re-measurement of the Kutch angles or positions, although unpublished re-measurements for mapping and control purposes are available in government archives that may now be available. Subsequent to the earthquake several Indian groups of geodesists from the Indian Institute of Geomagnetism (II G), the Indian Institute of Technology Bombay (IITB), the Centre for Mathematical Modelling & Computer Simulation (CMMACS), Bangalore, and the Wadia Institute of Himalayan Geology, Dehra Dun, undertook a series of measurements in the Kutch region. A subset of measurement points was measured by these several groups. The measured points extend approximately

100 km east, west and south of the epicentre. The GPS data are currently being processed to determine co-seismic changes during the earthquake. However, the number of GTS control points currently recovered is insufficient to constrain more than simple subsurface dislocation geometries.

Isoseismal Intensities

A full compilation of shaking effects for the 2001 earthquake will not be available for some time but the compiled news accounts from the immediate aftermath of the earthquake have been interpreted to obtain Modified Mercalli Intensities (MMI) at over 180 locations throughout India and Pakistan. Maps of the resulting intensity distribution are generated using a simple mathematical approach to interpolate between locations with known intensity values. Being away from the constrained data points, the maps do not reflect geologic site conditions, which influence shaking levels substantially. Previously the largest recorded intraplate earthquake in India occurred in 1897 and its magnitude (M=8. 1± 0.1) was determined only recently from the sparse global seismic network of the time and from geodetic estimates of seismic moment. The 1967 Me"6.5 Koyna intraplate earthquake was not felt sufficiently far from the epicentre to calibrate the far-field perceived intensity scale. The magnitudes of numerous other Indian earthquakes are known only from their intensity distributions, and an accurate attenuation versus distance relationship for Modified Mercalli Intensities on the Indian carton is currently unavailable.

For the first time, the seismological community will be able to estimate the attenuation of acceleration across the Indian carton using intensity observations from an intraplate Me"7.6 earthquake with a well-resolved instrumental magnitude. Although strong-motion accelerograph recordings of the Bhuj earthquake are sparse, we anticipate that the distribution of strong motion instruments in India will be adequate to calibrate Modified Mercalli Intensity (MMI) values relative to acceleration and frequency data. Isoseismal intensities provide an important data set with which to initiate this study. Armed with a newly calibrated attenuation curve, we anticipate that we will be able re-evaluate intensity data from historic Indian earthquakes in order to refine their estimated magnitudes. Results from the Bhuj earthquake may also provide a critical calibration for events that occurred in similar tectonic settings worldwide, including the 1811-1812 New Madrid earthquake. Although preliminary, the intensity maps already show several interesting features. The event was felt only lightly at the higher-elevation cities on Deccan lavas throughout central and southern India. Away from the Kutch region, intensities were clearly amplified significantly in areas that are along rivers, within deltas, or on coastal alluvium. One example is the Narmada River Valley in the province of Madhya Pradesh, where MMI values up to VI were reached at distances of over 600 km. Significant side effects were also observed within Mumbai. Most of the city experienced shaking at the MMI V level, but intensities of VI-VII were reached in areas built on landfill in southern and central Mumbai as well as along Bombay Harbour.

Implications for Future Hazard: India and Beyond

The 2001 Bhuj earthquake has important implications for earthquake hazards, not only in India, but also in other parts of the world where the source zones and/or the wave travel paths are similar. The occurrence of the Bhuj earthquake less than 200 years after the severe 1819 event provides further evidence that large intraplate earthquakes can occur in clusters in regions of the crust where the strain rate is relatively low. The event highlights the potential hazard faced by areas that lie outside more rapidly deforming plate boundary regions. The parallels between Kutch earthquakes and the 1811-1812 New Madrid earthquakes are remarkable. All of these earthquakes occurred within failed rift systems. The largest New Madrid earthquake may also have been similar in size to the Bhuj event. A recent reinterpretation of the February 7, 1812 New Madrid event obtained an Mw7.5. Previous studies had inferred Mw values as high as 8.0. Finally, both the Bhuj and the largest New Madrid event occurred on thrust faults favourably oriented for slip in the current stress regime that failed to produce either extensive or pronounced surface ruptures.

The distribution of shaking intensity in the Bhuj and New Madrid earthquakes was remarkably similar. Both events were felt at coastal regions as much as 2000 km from the epicentre, both caused light damage at sediment sites as far as 600 km away, and both generated substantial liquefaction over an extremely broad region. A thorough analysis of shaking effects from the Bhuj earthquake may help us better constrain the magnitude of the New Madrid earthquakes.

Since 1819 the population has increased by a factor of ten in Gujarat, and seismic resistant building codes have been implemented. Yet in 1819, 2000 people were killed, and in 2001 close to 20,000. It is difficult to escape the grim observation that the same fraction of the Kutch population lost their lives in the two earthquakes. Yet the long-term legacy of the Bhuj earthquake need not only be one of tragedy if the seismological and earthquake engineering communities can exploit the available data to the fullest extent possible and make use of the lessons learned. The Bhuj earthquake provides an important opportunity to better understand the hazard posed by earthquakes that occur in or affect intracratonic regions.

Some of the deadliest earthquakes

1556: Shaanxi, China

The deadliest quake of all time might be one of the least talked about, considering it occurred nearly 450 years ago. Centered in China's central Shaanxi province, the 1556 quake claimed the lives of some 830,000 people. The massive death toll is to be blamed only to the quake's strength (8.0 on the Richter scale, or more than 30 times more powerful than the recent quake in Haiti) as well as timing and location. The pre-modern structures were utterly unable to withstand a quake of such force, and massive landslides contributed to the casualties. An area some 500 miles wide was wiped out.

1908: Messina, Italy

By today's standards, the earthquake that struck beneath the Messina Strait — which separates the regions of Sicily and Calabria — on December 28, 1908, was of magnitude 7.5. A subsequent tsunami sent waves as much as 40 feet high crashing into the Italian coast. More than 80,000 people were killed and dozens of towns destroyed. Refugees from Messina were relocated to cities throughout Italy. Many were eventually transported to North America, aboard ships like the *Florida* — which, before reaching New York City, collided with another vessel, killing three already traumatized Italian passengers.

1920: Haiyuan, China

The December16, 1920 Haiyuan earthquake — which registered a 7.8 magnitude on the Richter scale — caused rivers to change course and sent landslides pouring down mountains. Destruction stretched across seven Chinese provinces. Sujiahe, a town in in Xiji County, was completely buried under a landslide. An estimated 200,000 people died in the disaster, which was felt as far away as Norway.

1923: Kanto, Japan

Shortly before noon on September 1, 1923, an earthquake measuring 7.9 on the Richter scale sent shockwaves through the Tokyo-Yokohama metropolitan area. The violent tremors left few buildings habitable and prompted a tsunami that surged up to 40 ft. (12 m.) high. But the damage continued for days: by the time the fires stemming from the quake were contained, 90% of Yokohama's buildings were reportedly damaged or were in ruins, and some two-fifths of Tokyo's buildings had been destroyed — leaving half its population homeless. Nearly 143,000 people died.

1948: Turkmenistan

In a matter of minutes, an October earthquake of magnitude 7.3 turned the city of Ashgabat into a pile of rubble. A thousand Soviet doctors, nurses and other medical personnel flooded in from Moscow and other cities to aid sufferers in what is now Turkmenistan. Despite their efforts, 110,000 people perished

1970: Chimbote, Peru

The Great Peruvian Earthquake hit the coastal town of Chimbote, Peru on May 31, 1970 — measuring 7.9 on the Richter scale. The epicentre of the quake was 15 miles away from the city, in the Pacific Ocean, yet the disaster claimed the lives of some 70,000 people and left more than 800,000 homeless. Landslides, with debris travelling at speeds of up to 200 mph down the sides of the Navado Huascaran mountain, destroyed whole villages. Tremors could be felt in Lima — some 400 miles away.

1976: Tangshan, China

China has the misfortune to have had the second deadliest earthquake on record, the 1976 Great Tangshan Earthquake, which struck the country's northeast. It would be more accurate to call this a binary quake: an aftershock that struck 16 hours after the initial temblor measured an identical 7.8 on the Richter scale and was equally destructive. Death estimates are hard to pin down — initial reports placed the toll at nearly 700,000, but those have since been revised down to some 250,000. Compounding the massive casualty count was the decision by the Chinese government to accept no international aid in the aftermath of the quakes.

Izmit: The 1999 Turkish earthquakes

On August 17, 1999 a heavy earthquake measuring 7. 5 on the Richter scale hit Izmit, a city in Turkey. It occurred on one of the world's longest and best-studied horizontal motion faults, called the east-west trending North Anatolian fault. This fault causes earthquakes at less than 20 km depth, bringing people at the surface close to where the energy is released.

The earthquake killed some 17,000 people and left thousands more without home. On November 12, another tremor of 7.2 on the Richter scale hit the location, killing 450 more and leaving 3000 people injured. Survivors of the earthquake were put together in temporary camps. Water transports were set up to prevent more people dying of dehydration. Fear of epidemics in these camps was very high.

The earthquake caused considerable environmental damage because it set fire to a refinery storing 700,000 tons of oil. By the time the fire burned out air, land and water were polluted. According to Greenpeace, the earthquake caused cracks in the Petkim waste dump, exposing chemical waste that was dumped there for years. A PVC factory, waste treatment plant and incinerator were also damaged. Fortunately, despite all these events of pollution, damages to the environment were limited by the cleanup operation.

Turkey has had a long history of earthquakes. In 1939 and 1967 earthquakes had already occurred on the North Anatolian fault, but these were not as strong as the first 1999 earthquake. The earthquake was the strongest the world had experienced for more than a decade, particularly because of the high death toll. The 2004 Asian earthquake now surpasses this.

2005: Pakistan-occupied Kashmir

Kashmir, the site of a prolonged and violent border dispute between India and Pakistan, is beleaguered enough; a massive earthquake on Oct. 8, 2005 only added to the province's woes. Measuring 7.6 on the Richter scale, the quake killed 79,000 and left millions more homeless. The remote, mountainous terrain compounded problems for rescue and recovery efforts, as crews struggled to reach the injured.

2008: Sichuan Province, China

Over 87,000 people died in China's deadly 2008 earthquake, and an estimated 10 million were left homeless. The 7.9-magnitude disaster struck the mountainous Sichuan province in western China, destroying millions of buildings and causing an estimated $86 billion worth of damage. Nearly 10,000 children died in schools — trapped under rubble when the buildings collapsed — leading to public outcry and a government investigation that found that as many as 20 percent of primary schools may have been shoddily constructed and unsafe. Grieving parents' initial calls for justice, however, have been silenced to a large extent by intimidation and alleged payoffs.

Chapter – 3

Tsunami

Tsunamis are one or a series of huge sea waves caused by submarine (underwater) earth movements that may result from earthquakes, landslides, volcanic eruptions and large meteorite impacts. The submarine earth movement occurs following a sudden change in the relative position of underwater tectonic plates. So, a tsunami may be defined as a sea wave of local or distant origin that results from large-scale seafloor displacements associated with large earthquakes, major submarine slides, or exploding volcanic islands. In simple words, we can say tsunamis are vast sea waves caused by the sudden dropping or rising of a section of the sea floor following earthquakes, landslides, volcanic eruptions and large meteorite impacts.

Tsunamis occur frequently in Japan. The word *tsunami* comes from Japanese. Literally, it means 'harbor wave.' It is composed of the two *kanji* characters *tsu* meaning '**harbor**' and *nami*, meaning '**wave**'. (*Kanji* are the adopted Chinese characters that are used in the modern Japanese writing system.) In Japanese, the word *tsunami* is used both as singular and as plural. However, in English the word *tsunamis* may be used as plural.

Many early geological, geographical, and oceanographic texts refer to tsunamis as **seismic sea waves**. Tsunamis are potentially the most catastrophic of all ocean waves. Tsunamis may reach enormous dimensions and have sufficient energy to travel across entire oceans. The power of a tsunami can be enhanced and fed by lunar positioning and boundaries that focus its energy. Tsunamis travel rapidly across deep ocean basins (about 480 mph!) and can grow to heights of tens of metres as they enter shallow water and approach shore. Owing to the immense volumes of water and the high energy involved, tsunamis can devastate coastal regions.

A tsunami may be as much as 30 metres high and 200 kilometres long, and may continue to occur for as long as a few days. A tsunami is barely discernible in the open ocean due to its low height or amplitude. But its amplitude may increase greatly as it approaches shallow coastal waters. They typically have periods greater than 10 minutes.

Some meteorological conditions, such as deep depressions that cause tropical cyclones, can generate a storm surge, called a **meteotsunami**, which can raise tides several metres above normal levels. The displacement comes from low atmospheric pressure within the centre of the depression. As these storm surges reach shore, they may resemble (though are not) tsunamis, inundating vast areas of land.

Etymology and History

Tsunamis are sometimes referred to as tidal waves. In recent years, this term has fallen out of favour, especially in the scientific community, because tsunamis actually have nothing to do with tides. Description of tsunamis as tidal waves is based on their most common appearance, which is that of an extraordinarily high tidal bore. Tsunamis and tides both produce waves of water that move inland, but in the case of a tsunami the inland movement of water is much greater and lasts for a longer period, giving the impression of an incredibly high tide. Unlike tides, tsunamis are not limited to harbours, therefore geologists and oceanographers discourage the use of the term tidal waves for tsunamis.

There are only a few other languages that have an equivalent native word. In the Tamil language, the word is *aazhi peralai*. In the Acehnese language, it is *ië beuna* or *alôn buluëk* (depending on the dialect). Note that in the fellow Austronesian language of Tagalog, a major language in the Philippines, *alon* means 'wave'. On the Simeulue island, off the western coast of Sumatra in Indonesia, in the Defayan language the word for tsunami is *smong*, while in the Sigulai language it is *emong*.

As early as 426 BC the Greek historian Thucydides inquired in his book *History of the Peloponnesian War* about the causes of tsunami, and was the first to argue that ocean earthquakes must be the cause. He wrote: "The cause of this phenomenon must be sought in the earthquake. At the point where its shock has been the most violent the sea is driven back, and suddenly recoiling with redoubled force, causes the inundation. Without an earthquake I do not see how such an accident could happen."

The Roman historian Ammianus Marcellinus described the typical sequence of a tsunami, including an incipient earthquake, the sudden retreat of the sea and a following gigantic wave, after the 365 AD tsunami devastated Alexandria. While Japan may have the longest recorded history of tsunamis, the sheer destruction caused by the 2004 earthquake and tsunami event mark it as the most devastating of its kind in modern times, killing around 230,000 people. The Sumatran region is not unused to tsunamis either, with earthquakes of varying magnitudes regularly occurring off the coast of the island.

Tsunami Generation Mechanisms

The principal generation mechanism (or cause) of a tsunami is the displacement of a substantial volume of water or perturbation of the sea. This displacement of water is usually attributed to either earthquakes, landslides, volcanic eruptions, glacier calvings or more rarely by meteorites and nuclear tests. The waves formed in this way are then sustained by gravity. Tides do not play any part in the generation of tsunamis. Tsunami can be generated when the sea floor abruptly deforms and vertically displaces the overlying water. Tectonic earthquakes are a particular kind of earthquake that are associated with the earth's crustal deformation. When these earthquakes occur beneath the sea, the water above the deformed area is displaced from its equilibrium position. More specifically, a tsunami can be generated when thrust faults associated with convergent or destructive plate boundaries move abruptly, resulting in water displacement, owing to the vertical component of movement involved. Movement on normal faults will also cause displacement of the seabed, but the size of the largest of such events is normally too small to give rise to a significant tsunami.

Tsunamis have a small amplitude (wave height) offshore, and a very long wavelength (often hundreds of kilometers long as compared to a wavelength of only 30 or 40 metres of normal ocean waves). That is why tsunamis generally pass unnoticed at sea, forming only a slight swell usually about 300 millimetres (12 inches) above the normal sea surface. They grow in height when they reach shallower water, in a wave shoaling process. A tsunami can occur in any tidal state and even at a low tide can inundate coastal areas.

Examples of tsunami originating at locations away from convergent boundaries include Storegga about 8,000 years ago, Grand Banks (1929), Papua New Guinea (1998) and Tappin (2001). The Grand Banks and Papua New Guinea tsunamis came from earthquakes which destabilized sediments, causing them to flow into the ocean and generate a tsunami. They dissipated before travelling transoceanic distances. The cause of the Storegga sediment failure is unknown. Possibilities include an overloading of the sediments, an earthquake or a release of gas hydrates (methane etc.)

The 1960 Valdivia earthquake (M_w 9.5) (19:11 hrs UTC), 1964 Alaska earthquake (M_w 9.2), 2004 Indian Ocean earthquake (M_w 9.2) (00:58:53 UTC) and 2011 Tôhoku earthquake (M_w9.0) are recent examples of powerful megathrust earthquakes that generated tsunamis (known as *teletsunamis*) that can cross entire oceans. Smaller (M_w 4.2) earthquakes in Japan can trigger tsunamis (called *local* and *regional tsunamis*) that can devastate nearby coasts in only a few minutes.

In the 1950s, it was discovered that larger tsunamis than had previously been believed possible could be caused by giant landslides. These phenomena rapidly displace large water volumes, as energy from the falling debris or expansion transfers to the water at a rate faster than the water can absorb. Their existence was confirmed in 1958 when a giant landslide in Lituya Bay, Alaska, caused the highest wave ever recorded, which had a height of 524 metres (over 1700 feet). The wave did not travel far, as it struck land almost immediately. Two people fishing in the bay were killed, but another boat amazingly managed to ride the wave. Scientists named these waves *megatsunami*. Scientists discovered that extremely large landslides from volcanic island collapses can generate megatsunamis that can cross oceans.

A tsunami warning is generally automatically issued after an earthquake of Richter 6.8 offshore Alaska, or Richter 7.5 offshore the western US or British Columbia. A 'warning' means immediate evacuation of low-lying areas is required. A 'watch' means a warning may follow. Authorities will cancel watches and warnings whenever sufficient information permits the decision. Emergency workers and the news media must know (1) the difference between a watch and a warning, and (2) that a tsunami may consist of several waves over several hours. It is not, repeat tidal wave, but a huge destructive wave

Major Tsunami Disasters

As already stated, tsunami is a series of waves in the ocean or sea and it can create a lot of havoc and destruction in the areas affected. It can also cause by a volcanic eruption beneath the surface of water. Energy generated by an earthquake under the water is released in the form of a series of waves. The waves are very powerful and can brush off everything that comes in the way. Tsunamis occurring in deep oceans are not as destructive, and do not rise much. But the one that is generated nearer the coasts causes giant waves to form and cause more destruction. Let us discuss some of the major tsunamis of all times:

Tsunami of Lisbon, Portugal

In 1755, Lisbon, Portugual, around 9:30 in the morning was hit by an earthquake of a Richter 9 magnitude. The core was the west-southwest of Cape St. Vincent, situated in the Atlantic Ocean. There were three earthquake shakes; the shakes were so strong that they created 16 feet cracks in the earth. After 30 minutes, more destruction followed, when a tsunami hit the coast of Portugal. Two more tsunami waves followed. The waves almost reached as high as 98 feet. Eighty-five percent of buildings in Lisbon had been destroyed and over 100,000 people were killed.

Tsunami in Sanriku, Japan

On 15 June, 1896, an earthquake occurred the northeast coast of Honshu Island, some 90 miles from the shore. It measured 8.5 on the Richter scale, followed by a gigantic tsunami, hitting the northeast coast of Japan. There is not much knowledge available about the earthquake doing an overwhelming damage though 26,000 people were killed.

Tsunami Messina, Italy

On the early morning of 28 December, 1908, Messina in Italy witnessed the deadliest earthquake in the European history. The earthquake was of 7.2 magnitude, bringing down several high buildings and burying many people in it. Few moments later, the tsunami came, with wave height between 20 to 40 feet. The entire city of Messina was shook . Out of a 150,000 total population almost 100,000 people had been killed or suffered huge destruction in the earthquake and tsunami disaster.

Tsunami of Kamchatka Peninsula, Russia

On 4 November, 1952, an earthquake hit the coast of the Kamchatka peninsula, Russia, leading to a tsunami. The earthquake measured 8.2 on the Richter scale with the focal depth of 30 km. Six cows died and loss ranged from $800,000 to $1,000,000 in Hawaii, and no human loss was recorded. The tsunami caused severe damage to Kamchatka peninsula, flooding streets and buildings. In the Hawaiian islands, boats were destroyed, telephone lines were knocked down and lawns were flooded. Other damage included a cement barge thrown and a bridge connecting the Cocoanut Island to the shore was destroyed.

Tsunami in South Central Chile

On 22 May, 1960, the strongest earthquake was recorded in the history near the coast of South Central Chile. It measured 9.5 on the Richter scale. Just 15 minutes after the earthquake a tsunami came with a height of 30 feet. It flooded more than 500 miles of the Chilean coast. The earthquake together with tsunami and mudslide damages caused $550 million recorded loss and around 2,000 people died.

Tsunami of Izmit Bay, Turkey

On 17 August, 1999, an earthquake of Richter 7.6 magnitude struck near the Izmit Bay, northwestern Turkey. It lasted for almost 37 seconds, killing around 40,000 to 45,000 people and approximately half a million people were left homeless.

The city of Izmit was damaged badly. There was an increased in number of deaths the following winter. The condition was very poor as the survivors were living in unprotected shelters and even on the street. About 50,000 houses were damaged to the highest degree, 2,000 buildings collapsed and 4,000 buildings were badly damaged, leaving 600,000 people homeless.

Tsunami in the Indian Ocean

On 26 December, 2004 a 9.2 Richter magnitude earthquake rocked the bottom of the Indian Ocean, releasing energy equivalent to that of 23,000 atomic bombs. The largest earthquake in 40 years, it was named the Sumatra-Andaman earthquake because its epicentre was near the west coast of the Indonesian island of Sumatra. It triggered a destructive tsunami across the Indian Ocean, sending a series of waves as high as 30 metres crashing onto the shores of 11 countries in eastern Asia. Within hours, the coasts of Indonesia, India, Sri Lanka, Thailand, and other countries, were overflowing with waves, as high as 49 feet. Over 310,000 people were killed in a dozen countries. This earthquake is now known as one of the most deadly disasters of modern history. The people dead in this tsunami were more than eight times than in any other tsunami. More than one-third of the people dead were children. Some people were swept out to sea while others drowned in their homes, unable to escape. According to the US Geological Survey, the official death toll was 227,898.

The earthquake was among the 10 deadliest in history. Scientists reported that it had lasted nearly ten minutes when most major earthquakes last no more than a few seconds. Since 1900, the only earthquakes recorded with a greater magnitude were the 1960 Great Chilean Earthquake (9.5), the 1964 earthquake in Prince William Sound (9.2), and the 1957 earthquake near the Andreanof Islands (9.1). But all these areas were less densely populated than the Asian area struck by the 2004 earthquake and therefore had a much smaller death toll.

The 2004 earthquake caused the entire planet to vibrate at least a few centimetres. It also triggered earthquakes in faraway regions, such as Alaska.

The earthquake triggered a a series of tsunami of more than 30 metres high, which washed ashore. It caused in serious damage and killed people in Sri Lanka, South India, Thailand, Indonesia, Somalia, Myanmar, Malaysia, the Maldives and other countries. The official death toll of 227,898 of the Asian earthquake is surpassed only by an earthquake in China in 1557, which killed over 830,000 people.

The 2004 tsunami not only impacted humans but also the environment. Severe damage was inflicted on ecosystems such as coral reefs, sand dunes and rock formations, animal and plant biodiversity and groundwater. In addition, the spread of solid and liquid waste and industrial chemicals polluted the water. The destruction of sewage collectors and treatment plants posed a serious threat to the environment. The United Nations Environment Program (UNEP), which works with local governments to determine ecological damage and frame appropriate policy measures, termed the tsunami relief operations the costliest ever. The restoration of the damaged area was estimated to take between 5 and 10 years.

In 2006, the Tsunami Evaluation Coalition (TEC) released a report on the efficiency of international aid after the 2004 earthquake and tsunami in Asia. TEC is a cooperation between UN organisations such as Unicef and WHO, consultancies, donors and organisations for humanitarian aid such as Oxfam Novib.

The TEC report listed the main positive conclusions as:

- High efficiency of the first aid
- Rapid reconstruction of schools and health centres
- Rapid restoring of the fishery sector
- However, the TEC report stressed the need for improvement in the following areas:
- The quality of international aid, and support of large international organisations for small local organisations.
- A general lack of cooperation between organisations because of large funding.
- Unequal distribution of funding; first aid was more adequately funded, whereas more money was required for restoration.

- International organisations focus too much on promoting their own name, causing information transfer to be inefficient.
- Costs for housing and personnel were far too high.
- Disaster response quality should be improved, and this was not attended to so far.

Chapter – 4

Tornado

Tornado is a violently rotating column of air extending from a cumulonimbus cloud to the earth, ranging in width from a few metres to more than a kilometre. A tornado may whirl at speeds between 64 km (40 mi) and 509 km (316 mi) per hour or higher with comparable updrafts in the center of the vortex. The vortex may contain several smaller vortices rotating within it. A tornado typically takes the form of a twisting, funnel-shaped cloud extending downward from storm clouds, often reaching the ground, and dissolving into thin, ropelike clouds as the tornado dissipates. Tornadoes may travel from a few dozen metres to hundreds of kilometres along the ground. Tornadoes usually form in the tail end of violent thunderstorms, with weaker funnels sometimes forming in groups along a leading *squall line* of an advancing cold front or in areas near a *hurricane*. The strongest tornadoes, which may last several hours and travel hundreds of kilometres, can cause massive destruction in a relatively narrow strip along their path. The causes of tornado formation are not well understood.

The Fujita Scale

Like earthquake, the strength of a tornado is measured according to a scale called Fujita scale. The scale was introduced in 1971 by Theodore Fujita of the University of Chicago and Allan Pearson, head of the Forecast Center in Kansas City, Missouri. It is based on the intensity by the damage it inflicts on human-built structures. The actual F scale of a tornado is determined after it has hit, according to satellite images, eye-witness accounts and visible damage. The Fujita scale divides tornadoes in six separate categories, as listed in Table 1.

Table 1: *Tornadao categories according to the Fujita tornado scale*

Scale number	Wind speed (Km/h)	Damage
F1	73-115	Light — Broken tree branches and some damage to chimneys
F2	116-180	Considerable — Roofs of houses blown and cars lifted slightly
F3	181-250	Severe — Walls damaged, cars fully lifted and most trees uprooted
F4	251-330	Devastating — Cars and badly constructed houses thrown around
F5: Twister	331-415	Incredible — Strong frame houses levelled off foundations and swept away, automobile-sized missiles fly away in excess of 100 metres
F6: Super twister	416-510	Inconceivable — Top end of F5 category

Mid-November 2006 Tornado Outbreak

In the recent history, a significant tornado outbreak occurred across the southern United States and into the mid-Atlantic states on November 15 and 16, 2006. It is termed as mid-November 2006 tornado outbreak. It took place along a sharp cold front that tracked across the entire region from west to east. At least nine people were killed by the many tornadoes that damaged many communities. The bulk of the tornadoes occurred on November 15, but the deadliest tornado took place on the morning of November 16 in southern North Carolina. A moderate risk of severe weather was issued by the Storm Prediction Center for a large section of the southeast for the night of the November 14 into November 15. The activity started in the overnight hours in Louisiana and Arkansas and tracked eastward, producing scattered tornadoes across the entire gulf coast and into the Carolinas over the next 36 hours. The most severe tornadoes took place in St. Helena Parish, Louisiana where one person was killed in a mobile home, Sumrall, Mississippi where an F3 tornado led to severe damage and numerous injuries, and in Montgomery, Alabama where an indoor roller skating park was destroyed with 30 children inside (but no serious injuries). When the line crossed into Georgia and northern Florida, it formed into a squall line. However, breaks in the squall line allowed super cells to form in the overnight hours, and early on the 16th, the deadly tornado in southern North Carolina formed at the end of the outbreak. In total, 28 tornadoes were confirmed. Following are some details of the destruction caused by the mid-November 2006 tornado outbreak.

Louisiana: The tornado hit Amite area in St. Helena, Tangipahoa. Intermittent touchdown in the area. Mobile home destroyed along Highway 441. Major damage was also reported in the rural area to several houses. One death was reported and two people were injured.

Franklinton area in Washington: Three houses sustained structural damage in the area, one of them was heavily damaged.

Mississippi: Sumrall area in Lamar, Forrest. Severe tornado touchdown in the community. Extensive structural damage to 25 houses, 16 of which were destroyed. Enormous damage to trees and power lines was also reported along a 500 yard (450 m) wide path.

The most severe damage involved a wood frame house that was flattened. Six people were injured.

Dexter area in Walthall, Marion: 16 buildings were damaged, many of them severely. One person was injured in a mobile home.

SE of Laurel in Jones, Wayne: Significant damage to 25 houses. Two mobile homes, one being used as temporary housing after Hurricane Katrina, were flattened. Extensive tree damage was also reported. Two electric transmission towers were knocked down along a half-mile (800 m) wide path. A few minor injuries were reported.

E of Laurel in Jones: Related to the main Laurel area tornado. Damage limited to trees.

NW of Purvis in Lamar: One outbuilding was destroyed and a shed lost its roof. Extensive tree damage.

Sand Hill in Greene: At least eight houses and part of a church were damaged. Extensive damage to trees and power lines.

Arkansas: The affected area was Brinkley in Monroe. Damage was reported to about 50 houses and businesses. Four silos and an outbuilding were destroyed. Extensive tree and power line damage.

Chatom in Washington: Several homes suffered roof damage. Horse barn damaged.

Pintlala in Lowndes, Montgomery: Significant damage reported, especially around Pintlala Elementary School. Overall damage moderate to heavy, with numerous houses, the school and a church damaged along US 31.

Alabama: The affected area was Montgomery in Montgomery. Heavy damage reported in the east end of Montgomery. The Fun Zone Skate Center was destroyed with over 30 children inside. Fortunately, they all escaped with only a few minor injuries. Other houses and businesses were also damaged, including a postal distribution center. Extensive tree and power line damage.

NE of Eclectic in Elmore: Damage to trees and power lines south of Lake Martin. One house lost its roof.

SE of Wetumpka in Elmore: One house was damaged and saw its roof shift. Some tree damage was reported.

W of Reeltown in Tallapoosa: Minor damage to a mobile home and three outbuildings, also some tree damage reported.

W of Opp in Covington: Significant damage was reported along the track. Numerous houses lost their roofs. Several farms were destroyed, with the most severe damage located at six poultry farms, where over 130,000 chickens were killed and the farms were all destroyed.

Hamilton Crossroads area in Pike, Barbour: Significant damage reported in the area. Several houses lost their roofs and numerous mobile homes were destroyed. The local fire department building collapsed and the water tower crashed to the ground.

Lafayette in Chambers: Heavy damage to a service station and a storage shed.

Mount Andrew in Barbour: One house sustained roof and wall damage from this brief touchdown.

Dyas in Baldwin: A house on the east side of Dyas road sustained considerable roof damage. In addition, two sheds, one barn, one horse pen, and a screened in porch were destroyed at the residence.

Georgia: The affected area was Fort Benning in Chattahoochee, Muscogee. Significant tornado touchdown in the army base. About 20 large warehouses were damaged, and 6 houses were destroyed along its 1/4 mile (400 m) wide path. Six people suffered minor injuries.

North Carolina: The affected area was Cramerton in Gaston. Light damage was reported.

N of Lowesville in Lincoln: Short-lived tornado.

E of Denver in Lincoln: Substantial damage reported on the west side of Lake Norman.

E of Statesville in Iredell: One death was reported amid intermittent damage. Many trees were knocked down, some landing on mobile homes. Eight mobile homes were damaged. One man was critically injured when a refrigerator landed on him. He died in December from his injuries.

SE of Manning in Clarendon: Multiple touchdowns of tornado along its path, may have been one or multiple tornadoes. Tornado remained in rural areas with damaged limited to trees. Riegelwood area in Columbus, Pender: Eight deaths were reported.

Southern North Carolina Tornado

The deadliest tornado of the mid-November outbreak (2006) struck a primarily rural area in the Columbus county in southern North Carolina, just west of Wilmington, on the morning of November 16. It touched down at 6:37 am EST (1137 UTC), according to the Storm Prediction Center.

The tornado first touched down in the community of Riegelwood, where the most significant damage was reported. The most devastating impact took place in a mobile home park, resulting in at least eight deaths and 20 injuries, of which at least five were in critical condition after the tornado hit. At least 30 houses were destroyed and some were flattened. At the peak of the storm, 40,000 people were without electricity; most of them were quickly restored. The tornado was 300 yards (270 m) wide at its widest point and was confirmed as an F3 on the Fujita scale for about one mile.

The tornado continued eastward for 7 miles (11 km) as a much weaker and narrower tornado with F1 damage. Nonetheless, as it tracked into Pender county, three more houses were damaged before it dissipated.

The 1925 Ellington, Missouri Tornado

The United States has a history of tornadoes, destroying homes and land and killing people on their way. About 80% of all tornadoes occur in the US, mostly on the Great Plains. A tornado consists of a rapidly rotating vortex of air that forms a funnel Tornadoes become harmful when the funnel touches earth. Winds of 250-300 km/h cause tornadoes to lift objects weighing hundreds of tons and may even drain entire lakes. Tornadoes typically cause destruction in areas 1 km wide and 10-20 km long.

In 1925, a particularly violent F5 scale tornado hit Ellington, Missouri in the United States and blew over a number of towns in Missouri, Illinois and even Indiana. This tornado had the highest death rate (see Table 2) and the highest number of destroyed buildings of all tornadoes in the US history. The tornado blew through a ridge where a series of mining towns were situated. These towns became the main targets of the devastating winds associated with the tornado.

The tornado was not very visible because of the large amount of dust present in the area. Low visibility and the great forward speed of the tornado caused many people to be surprised by its occurrence. This caused a high death toll in many different cities.

When the tornado hit West Frankfort most men were working in the mine. About 800 miners had to await a power failure before they could reach their homes. The 127 deaths and 450 injuries caused by the tornado were mostly among their women and children.

Table 2: Death toll of the Missouri tornado in various states/ towns

State	Town	Death toll
Missouri	Ellington	1
	Annapolis	2, 75 injured
	Perry County	1
	Bollinger County	32
	Other	13
Illinois	Gorham	34, the town was destroyed
	Desoto	69
	Murphysboro	234
	Parrish	22
	West Frankfort	127, 450 injured
	Hamilton/ Whit County	65
Indiana	Princeton	71

The Missouri tornado is currently the number one United States tornado with the highest death toll and the most violent winds. In total, it killed 671 people and injured another 2,027.

Other tornadoes

Tornadoes have occurred all over the United States for many centuries. Some of the major tornadoes are listed below:

1. **1840** Natchez: 317 dead, 109 injured
2. **1869** St. Louis: 255 dead, 1000 injured
3. **1884** Great Southern Tornadoes (60): 170 dead
4. **1890** Louisville: 125 dead
5. **1899** New Richmond: 117 dead, 200 injured
6. **1908** Texas/Georgia: 320 dead, 770 injured
7. **1913** Omaha, Nebraska: 94 dead, 350 injured
8. **1920** Mississippi/Alabama: 224 dead
9. **1927** Missouri/Arkansas/Texas: 217 dead
10. **1932** Alabama/Georgia/Tennessee: 330 dead
11. **1936** Tupelo, Mississippi: 216 dead, 700 injured

12. **1936** Gainesville, Georgia: 203 dead, 1.600 injured
13. **1944** West Virginia: 144 dead
14. **1945** Oklahoma: 102 dead
15. **1947** Texas/Oklahoma/ Kansas: 181 dead, 970 injured
16. **1952** Arkansas: 208 dead
17. **1953** Waco: 114 dead, 597 injured
18. **1953** Flint: 115 dead, 844 injured
19. **1955** Udall, Kansas: 115 dead (half of population)
20. **1965** Palm Sunday Outbreak: 271 dead
21. **1966** Mississippi/Alabama: 61 dead
22. **1971** Mississippi Delta Outbreak: 119 dead, 1000 injured
23. **1974** Xenia, Ohio: 350 dead
24. **1979** Wichita Falls: 60 dead, 1.740 injured
25. **1984** Carolina: 67 dead, 1.248 injured
26. **1994** Georgia/South Carolina: 42 dead, 320 injured
27. **1999** Texas/Oklahoma/ Kansas: 45 dead, 775 injured

Typhoon Xangsane

Typhoon Xangsane (international designation: 0615, JTWC designation: 18W, PAGASA name: Typhoon Milenyo) was a deadly typhoon that affected the Philippines, Vietnam, and Thailand during the 2006 Pacific typhoon season. It was the fifteenth tropical storm and ninth typhoon recognized by the Japan Meteorological Agency operationally during the season, although in post-operational analysis it became the tenth typhoon of the season with the addition of Typhoon Maria. According to the Joint Typhoon Warning Center, Xangsane was the sixteenth tropical storm and tenth typhoon of the season, and was a Category 4-equivalent typhoon in terms of 1-minute average wind speeds. The name Xangsane was submitted by Laos and means elephant.

Xangsane made landfall in the Philippines, battering the northern islands with torrential rains and strong winds, and causing widespread flooding and landslides. After passing over Manila and emerging over the South China Sea, the typhoon made a second landfall in central Vietnam, also causing flooding and landslides there and in Thailand. The storm was responsible for at least 279 deaths, mostly in the Philippines and Vietnam, and at least $747 million in damage.

Meteorological History of Typhoon Xangsane

Late on September 24, 2006, the Joint Typhoon Warning Center (JTWC), noted that an area of convection, had persisted about 460 NM to the southeast of Manila, in the Philippines. The JTWC assessed the development of a significant tropical cyclone as fair. This was because convection was beginning to flare up near a developing Low Level Circulation Center. The JTWC also noted that the disturbance had a broad circulation. Early next day both the Japan Meteorological Agency and the Philippine Atmospheric, Geophysical and Astronomical Services Administration (PAGASA) designated the tropical disturbance as a tropical depression with PAGASA assigning the local name of Tropical Depression Milenyo to the depression. Later that morning, the JTWC reassessed the potential of the disturbance forming into a significant tropical cyclone within 24 hours as good, and issued a tropical cyclone formation alert on the developing disturbance. Early that afternoon the JTWC started to issue advisories on the disturbance and designated it as Tropical Depression 18W. Later that day, as the depression moved towards the west, it was upgraded to a Tropical Storm by the JTWC. Early on September 26, the JMA also upgraded the depression to a tropical storm, and assigned the international name of Xangsane.

Later on September 26, the JMA upgraded Xangsane to a severe tropical storm, while six hours later both the JMA and the JTWC upgraded Xangsane to typhoon with the JTWC reporting wind speeds equivalent to a category one typhoon. Early next day Xangsane was upgraded to a category 2 typhoon and then over the next six hours Xangsane rapidly intensified into a category 4 typhoon with wind speeds of 115 kts (130 mph, 215 km/h). Meanwhile, the JMA reported that Xangsane had reached its peak wind speeds of 85 kts (100 mph, 155 km/h). Early that afternoon, the JTWC reported that Xangsane had reached its peak wind speeds of 125 kts (145 mph, 230 km/h).

Xangsane then passed through the Philippine islands, wreaking havoc and becoming the strongest typhoon to directly impact Metro Manila in eleven years. As it entered the South China Sea as a weak typhoon, it began to re-intensify, reaching its secondary peak strength shortly before landfall at Da Nang, Vietnam on October 1. The JTWC ceased advisories after landfall, while the JMA carried the storm inland until it was over Thailand as a tropical depression. It remained as a low pressure area over central Indochina on the JMA's weather charts for several days, while the US Navy's Automated Tropical Cyclone Forecasting system carried the remnants of Xangsane into the Bay of Bengal.

Vietnam

Prior to Xangsane's final landfall, the Vietnamese government set up a steering committee headed by Deputy Prime Minister Nguyen Sinh Hung to oversee evacuations and storm preparations throughout central Vietnam. Provincial and local authorities evacuated over 300,000 people from low-lying areas along the coast from Ha Tinh to Phu Yen, as well as hilly areas prone to landslides. The Vietnamese government also ordered about

2,400 boats, including 273 fishing boats, to return to port. Vietnam Airlines cancelled or diverted all flights on September 30 and October 1, 2006. These efforts were carried out in order to prevent a repeat of the damage and fatalities caused by Typhoon Chanchu earlier in the season. Xangsane made its second and final landfall in central Vietnam, causing severe flooding and strong winds that caused nearly 10 trillion Vietnamese dong ($629 million) in damage and killed 71 people. The worst structural damage occurred in the city of Da Nang, where 26 people were killed. The provinces of Quang Nam and Nghe An were also hard hit, with a total of 25 people killed. The storm damaged or destroyed around 320,000 homes, downed thousands of trees and power lines, and flooded major streets.

On October 3, the International Federation of Red Cross and Red Crescent Societies (IFRC) released 100,000 Swiss francs ($80,300) from its disaster relief fund to support the Red Cross of Vietnam, and issued an emergency appeal for 1 million Swiss francs ($810,000) in aid the next day. The Vietnamese government also released 100 billion Vietnamese dong ($6.2 million) and 1,500 metric tons (1,650 short tons) of rice from the national food security stock to help the recovery effort in central Vietnam. The National Fatherland Front also issued an appeal to national and international organizations for donations and aid.

Thailand

Although Xangsane had weakened considerably over land, residents of northern Thailand were advised of the threat of flooding from the remnant low of Xangsane as it approached. The Department of Disaster Prevention and Mitigation alerted its provincial offices throughout the country to be prepared for strong winds, flash flooding, and landslides. Residents in highland areas were also warned of possible mudslides, and the army was dispatched to aid in regional storm preparations.

The remnants of Xangsane moved over Thailand on October 2 and combined with monsoonal moisture over the north central part of the country, causing torrential rains and severe flooding in over 35 provinces. Floodwaters broke through levees and barriers and flooded or damaged nearly 1.3 million rai (2,100 km , 520,000 acres) of farmland and local infrastructure. Many municipalities reported flooding of up to three metres, and the municipality of Angthong reported flooding of 60 cm (2 ft). The Department of Disaster Prevention and Mitigation reported 47 deaths. Villages in several provinces reported significant levels of water pollution and waterborne illnesses from stagnant waters.

As a result of the deaths and damage caused, it was decided at the 39th annual meeting of the ESCAP/WMO Typhoon Committee in Manila in December 2006 that the name Xangsane, along with four others, would be retired from the name list. Its PAGASA name, Milenyo, was also retired by PAGASA. In December 2007, the committee selected the name Leepi to replace Xangsane on the western Pacific basin name lists beginning in 2008. In 2010 the name selected by PAGASA to replace Milenyo was Mario.

Philippines

Damage was widespread in the Philippines, particularly in Metro Manila, where the typhoon passed almost directly over. Power and water was lost in several provinces, while overflowing rivers caused flooding, landslides and made roads impassable. In some parts of the country, electricity was cut off for up to six days straight. Many trees and billboards were toppled by Xangsane, while Luzon suffered an island-wide power outage. Rough waters and seaport closures left at least

3,400 people and nearly 270 vehicles stranded in ports and terminals, mainly at the primary ferry crossing between Samar Island and Bicol region. Local and provincial officials described Xangsane as the worst typhoon to directly impact Manila since Typhoon Angela passed over the city eleven years ago. The Philippine government estimated that approximately 2 million people in 19 provinces were affected by Xangsane, which destroyed many homes and farms on its path through the islands. The local and regional Philippine National Red Cross chapters reported major damage in at least 116 municipalities, 12 cities, and a total of 1,295 barangays across the country. Torrential rains from Milenyo also caused flooding and landslides in Laguna, Cavite, and Quezon. Xangsane caused the destruction of the Calumpang Dam in the Municipality of Liliw, which channeled water to irrigation canals around the area. In all, Milenyo was responsible for 197 deaths and 5.9 billion Philippine pesos ($118 million) in damage, mostly to personal property and agriculture.

Following the passage of Xangsane, the IFRC issued an emergency request for 5.7 million Swiss francs ($4.6 million) to aid the Philippine Red Cross in its relief effort. In addition, the movement dispatched 3,000 workers and three disaster response teams to affected areas for search and rescue missions, damage assessments, and assistance to people affected by the typhoon. The Philippine Red Cross provided canned goods, rice, clothing, and personal hygiene items to over 6,300 families, and local volunteers provided assistance to people in shelters. The Spanish Red Cross, present since 1998 as a backup to the Philippine Red Cross, also sent officials, logistics equipment, and water purification systems to the more heavily affected areas to aid in disaster relief and damage assessments.

Hurricane Mitch

Tropical cyclones are a type of low pressure system which generally forms in the tropics. They are an important part of the atmospheric circulation system, which moves heat from the equatorial region toward higher latitudes. Tropical cyclones can be either tropical storms, typhoons or hurricanes, depending on the wind speed.

Hurricanes are tropical cyclones that develop an area of calm in the centre of the circulation. Surrounding this area is an area of 16-80 km wide where strong thunderstorms and winds circulate around the centre. The circulation route depends on the hemisphere. In the Southern Hemisphere it is clockwise, whereas in the Northern Hemisphere it is counter-clockwise. Hurricanes can achieve wind speeds of up to 305 km/h.

In 1998 the category 5 Hurricane Mitch caused devastation in Central America, gaining wind speeds of 290 km/h and killing more than 18,000 people. Most deaths were caused by floods resulting from heavy rains (90 cm) associated with the hurricane.

Mitch formed in the Atlantic near Africa and travelled north along the coasts of Nicaragua and Honduras. It headed west for some time before approaching the coast again and heading into central Honduras. Mitch weakened and entered Guatemala as a mere tropical depression, but it soon started to reorganize. It again became a hurricane when it reached Yucatan and Florida later and it was even tracked north of Great Britain. Most damage was done in Honduras and Nicaragua, but El Salvador and Guatemala also received significant damage. Total damage estimates are up to 5 billion US dollars.

Hurricane Mitch was the second destructive hurricane to hit Honduras after Fifi in 1974, which killed an estimated 8,000 people. Mitch was the deadliest hurricane in more than 200 years, and the second deadliest ever. The Great Hurricane of 1780 remains the deadliest to this day. The name Mitch was disregarded in 1999 and was replaced by Matthew in 2004.

The Saffir-Simpson hurricane scale

Hurricanes are ranked according to the Saffir-Simpson hurricane scale on the basis of wind speeds. The scale was developed in 1969 by civil engineer Herbert Saffir and National Hurricane Center director Bob Simpson. In terms of effects, the rankings are not absolute because any type of hurricane can inflict terrible damage, even if wind speeds are not very high relatively. If hurricanes with low wind speeds result in floods and landslides, damages are still considerable. Table 3 lists different categories in which the Saffir-Simpson hurricane scale classifies hurricanes on the basis of wind speeds.

Table 3: Hurricane categories according to the Saffir-Simpson hurricane scale

Category	Wind speed (km/h)	Effects
1	119-153	No real damage to buildings. Some coastal flooding.
2	154-177	Some roofing, door and window damage. Considerable damage to vegetation.
3	178-209	Destruction of mobile homes. More inland flooding damage.
4	210-249	Erosion and flooding of inland areas. Roofs are torn off.
5	>250	Complete roof failures and some complete building failures. Flooding and landslides. Usually mass evacuation is implemented.

Other hurricanes

There have been hurricanes all over the tropics for many centuries. Table 4 lists some major hurricanes that occurred between 1893 and 2004.

Table 4: Major hurricanes between 1893 and 2004

Atlantic	Canada	United States
Sea Islands hurricane (1893)	Saxby Gale (1869)	Florida Keys Hurricane (1919)
Yucatan Hurricane (1934)	Great August Gale (1934)	Palm Beach Hurricane (1949)
Hurricane Fifi (1974)	Hurricane Hazel (1954)	Hurricane Donna (1960)
Hurricane Gordon (1994)	The Perfect Storm (1991)	Hurricane Andrew (1992)
Hurricane Jeanne (2004)	Hurricane Juan (2003)	Hurricane Charley (2004)

The Beijing and Queensland Dust Storms

Estimates have shown that dust storms blow about 118 million metric tonnes of desert sand from Africa to the Northeast Amazon Basin in Brazil annually. Dust storms occur everywhere around the world. Their natural function is replacement of soils and carrying nutrients from one part of the globe to another. Iron and other nutrients are blown out to sea where they maintain marine ecosystems. Central and South American rain forests also receive vital nutrients from the Saharan dust storms.

Causes of dust storms include droughts and poor farming and grazing practices. Oxford University geography professor Andrew Goudie stated in 2001 that cars driving the Sahara are another possible cause of dust storm formation.

Dust storms have increased as a result of extensive deforestation and desertification in many regions. This has caused some countries to start forestation projects.

Sensitive or allergic people suffer from dust storms because these carry not only nutrients but also microbes and pollens. For most people, however, dust storms are mainly a nuisance because the visibility is decreased and all human possessions are covered in a thick layer of dust. Following is a brief description of the damage caused by the recent dust storms in China and Australia.

China: In 1998, a violent dust storm hit China's capital Beijing, darkening the skies. This was the worst dust storm in over a decade. Dust was blown from the Gobi desert near Mongolia into the city. At least 12 people went missing during the storm and power and water supplies were cut. Three Beijing construction workers were killed when strong winds blew iron wire and asphalt off the top of a two-storey building.

Residents ran for cover in the streets, using towels to cover their faces, and the city's busy traffic ground to a halt in most areas. On the most busy roads in the town, the visibility had decreased to only 500 metres.

Schools were closed in China, North Korea and even Russia after the dust storm started. In the capital of South Korea, Seoul, children and elderly people were advised to stay indoors to prevent breathing problems. About 35 domestic flights in Seoul were cancelled and 70 were called off.

In total, more than 100 million people were affected by the 2000 dust storm. It is said that the storm was caused by arid weather and prevailing winds, and by pasture ploughing. The government in China wants to try to prevent future dust storms from hitting Beijing by planting a green belt of trees around the capital.

Australia: In 2002, Queensland in Australia was hit by a violent desert storm, which shut down regional airports. The government urged residents to stay indoors. The visibility fell as low as 50 metres in regions with reduced vegetation cover. The dust storm was at least 6 km high at Chaleville, South Queensland and blew more than a million tonnes of dust into the region. Some claimed this was the worst dust storm witnessed in 20 years.

It was said the cause of the dust storm was a gusty southerly wind change moving over Queensland. Like in Beijing, people with asthma, children and elderly people were advised to stay indoors to prevent breathing problems. Cars were obligated to drive with dipped headlights on. Aviation forecasters stated that many airports were closed.

Other dust storms

Dust storms are fairly common. Even in Europe the results of a dust storm can sometimes be witnessed as a small dust layer on the tops of cars. Some of the major dust storms are listed below:

1. **1901** dust storm from the Sahara to Europe and the Ural Mountains
2. **1928** dust storm from Ukraine to Romania and Poland

3. **1930-1931** Dust Bowl in the Oklahoma Panhandle region, causing red snow on England and a mass exodus
4. **1930** dust storms in Midwestern United States
5. **2001** dust storm from Asia to the United States

Chapter – 5

Flood

The dictionary meaning of flood is an overflowing of water onto land that is normally dry. Flood is a temporary rise in water level as in a river or lake or along a sea coast, resulting in its spilling over and out of its natural or artificial confines onto the land that is normally dry. Floods are usually caused by excessive runoff from precipitation or snowmelt, or by coastal storm surges or other tidal phenomena. Floods are sometimes described according to their statistical occurrence. A fifty-year flood is a flood that has a magnitude which is reached at a particular location on average once every fifty years. In any given year, there is a two percent statistical chance of the occurrence of a fifty-year flood and a one percent chance of a hundred-year flood.

The Bihar Flood of 2008

The 2008 Bihar flood was one of the most disastrous floods in the history of India. A breach in the Kosi embankment near the Indo-Nepal border (at Kusha in Nepal) occurred on 18 August, 2008. The river changed course and inundated areas which had not experienced floods in many decades. Heavy monsoon rains and poor maintenance caused the breach in the Kosi embankment. Water passed through the breach at an estimated 129,800 cumecs (cubic metres per second), inundating hundreds of villages in northern Bihar. The flood affected over 2.3 million people. It submerged most of the Kosi alluvial fan area, which is very fertile and has a dense agrarian population.

The Kosi river's upper basin in southern Tibet and arid eastern Nepal drains some 60,000 km^2 of mountainous terrain, a region that tectonic forces are elevating by about 1 cm a year. If the erosion keeps pace with geologic uplift, an estimated 600 million cubic metres of sediment is estimated to be carried downstream annually. However, empirical measurements of the river's sediment load have yielded estimates of 100 million cubic metres annually, indicating that the area traversed by the river is rising. River gradient ranges from more than 10 metres/km for major upper tributaries in the mountains to as little as 6 cm/km as the lower Kosi nears the Ganges. As the gradient decreases in the plains, current slows and turbulence that holds sediments in suspension diminishes. Sediments settle out and are deposited on the riverbed. This process eventually raises a channel above the surrounding terrain. The river breaks out, seeking lower terrain, which it again proceeds to elevate by deposition.

On 18 August, 2008, following the embankment breach at Kusha (Nepal), the Kosi picked up an old channel it had abandoned over 100 years ago near the border with Nepal and India. On its new course, it submerged several districts of Nepal and India. Ninety-five percent of the Kosi's total flow was reported flowing through the new course. The worst affected districts included Supaul,

Araria, Saharsa, Madhepura, Purnia, Katihar, parts of Khagaria and northern parts of Bhagalpur, as well as adjoining regions of Nepal.

Bihar, one of the poorest states in India, faced a tremendous challenge with more than 15 lakhs people displaced, hundreds dead and most of the affected areas remaining under stagnant muddy waters for a long time. After the initial evacuation and emergency rescue operations initiated by the Indian army and other relief operations, the affected communities struggled hard to survive in the new surroundings, with each day posing new challenges. The relief camps were temporary and the refugees' needs were growing while the solution to such a crisis is still in the air.

Kosi: Sorrow of Bihar

Flooding causes enormous loss of life and material in India annually. The country is second in the world after Bangladesh in deaths due to flooding, accounting for one-fifth of global flooding deaths. The Kosi, called the "Sorrow of Bihar," is one of two major tributaries, the other river being the Gandak, draining the plains of north Bihar, the most flood-prone area of India.

The Kosi is is a trans-boundary river flowing through Nepal and India. It is one of the largest tributaries of the Ganges. Due to frequent changes in its course from Nepal to India, the Kosi has caused widespread human suffering in the past through flooding. Over the last 250 years, the Kosi has shifted its course over 120 kilometres (75 mi) from east to west. The Kosi's unstable course is attributed to the heavy silt it carries during the monsoon season.

In the Nepali language, the Kosi is called Saptakoshi for its seven Himalayan tributaries. Some rivers of the Kosi system, such as the Arun, the Sun Koshi and the Bhote Koshi, originate in the Tibet Autonomous Region of China.

The Kosi is the lifeline of the 'Mithila' region, spread over more than half of India's state of Bihar, and parts of adjoining Nepal. Along with its tributaries, the Kosi drains 29,400 km^2/11,400 sq mi in China (mainly the upper Arun basin north of the Mount Everest region), 30,700 km^2/11,900 sqmi in Nepal (the eastern part of the country), and 9,200 km^2/3,600 sq mi in India. The river basin is surrounded by the ridges, which separate it from the Yarlung Zangbo river in the north, the Gandaki in the west and the Mahananda in the east. The river is joined by major tributaries in the Mahabharat Range approximately 48 km (30 mi) north of the Indo-Nepal border. Below the outermost foothills (Shivaliks), the river has built up a megafan some 15,000 square kilometres (5,800 sq mi) in extent, breaking into more than twelve distinct channels with shifting courses due to flooding. Kamlâ, Bâghmati (Kareh) and Budhi Gandak are major tributaries of the Kosi in India, besides minor tributaries like Bhutahi Balân.

Geography

In Nepal, the Kosi basin is bordered on the west by the basins of the Gandaki and the Bagmati (draining Kathmandu Valley). The Kanchenjunga Himalayas are its eastern watershed. The Kosi has seven major tributaries: Sun Koshi, Tamakoshi, Tamba Koshi, Dudh Kosi, Indravati Likhu, Arun and Tamur. The Dudh Kosi joins the Sun Koshi at the Nepalese village of Harkapur. At Triveni the Sun Koshi from the west is joined by the Arun from the north (the Dudh Kosi and Arun encircle Mount Everest), then the Tamar from the east. The combined river becomes the *Saptakoshi*, literally "Seven Koshis". The Saptakoshi crosses the Lesser Himalaya or Mahabharat Range in a deep gorge some 10 km (6.2 mi) long. At Barâhkcetra in Nepal it emerges from the mountains and becomes the *Koshi*. After flowing another 58 km (36mi) it crosses into

Bihar, India, near Bhimnagar and after another 260 km (160 mi) joins the Ganges near Kursela. The river has a total length of 729 km (453 mi).

There are two national parks in the Kosi river basin:

- The Sagarmatha National Park, located in eastern Nepal, containing parts of the Himalayas and the southern half of Mount Everest;
- The Koshi Tappu Wildlife Reserve situated on the floodplains of the Sapta-Koshi River in eastern Nepal.

Legend

This Kosi is mentioned in the epic 'Mahabharata' as Kausiki, named after the sage Viswamitra, who is said to have attained the status of Vedic or 'Rishi' on its banks. Viswamitra was a descendant of sage Kusika. Viswamitra is credited with writing many well-known Vedic hymns on the Kosi banks where he had his hermitage. These Vedic hymns include the Mandala, the Rigveda and the Gayatri Mantra. Due to the famous Vedic hymns composed on its banks, the Kosi is also referred to as the River Om or the Song of the Ganga.

The Kosi is also called Kausika in Rigveda.

The Koshi (Kosi in Sanskrit) is associated with many ancient spiritual stories. It is mentioned in the Bal Kand section of Valmiki Ramayana as the Kausiki who is the form assumed by Satyavati after her death. Satyavati was the elder sister of Viswamitra, descendants of Kushak dynasty. In the Markendeya Purana, the Kosi is described as the primal force. Due to the violent nature of the Kosi during monsoon season, legend says that Parvati, the wife of Shiva, after defeating the demon Durg, became known as the warrior Goddess Durga who was transformed into Kaushiki. In Ramayana, the river Ganges is depicted as her elder sister.

According to Mahabharata epic, the God of death took the form of a woman and resides on the banks of the river to keep the growth of human population under check. The Kosi resonates with the folklore of Mithila region. The most important depictions of Kosi folklore are Kosi as a virgin absolutely care-free and full of energy and as a frustrated wife of old hermit Richeek wandering in the Himalayas. The Kosi is also invoked as the mother — 'Kosi Ma'. These images underline the contradiction inherent in the Kosi river as a source of life and death, prosperity and destruction; a mother and an enchanting virgin.

Cause of the Kosi Flooding

The Koshi has an average water flow (discharge) of 1,654 cubic metres per second (58,400 cu ft/s). During floods, it increases to as much as 18 times the average. The greatest recorded flood was 24,200 m^3/s (850,000 cu ft/s) on 24 August 1954. The Kosi Barrage has been designed for a peak flood of 27,014 m^3/s (954,000 cu ft/s)(2).

Extensive soil erosion and landslides in its upper catchment have resulted in the silt yield of the Kosi of about 19 m /ha/year (10 cu yd/acre/yr), one of the highest in the world. Of major tributaries, the Arun with its origins in Tibet brings the greatest amount of coarse silt in proportion to its total sediment load. The river is able to transport its heavy sediment load down the steep gradients and narrow gorges in the mountains and foothills where the gradient is at least ten metres per km. On the plains beyond Chatra, the gradient falls below one metre per km, even to as little as 6 cm per km as the river approaches the Ganges. Current slows and the sediment load settles out of the water to be deposited on an immense alluvial fan that has grown to an area of about 15,000 km . This fan extends some 180 km from its apex where it leaves the foothills, across the international border into Bihar state and on to the Ganges. Instead of a single well-defined channel, the river has numerous interlacing channels that shift laterally over the fan from time to time. Without sufficient channelisation, floods spread out very widely. The record flow of 24, 200 m /s is equivalent to water a metre deep and more than 24 km, flowing down the slight slope of the alluvial fan at one metre per second.

Glaciers, Glacier Lakes and GLOF

In the Himalayas, glaciers are melting and retreating, which results in formation of lakes insecurely dammed by ice or moraines. These dams are at risk of breaking, causing a glacial lake outburst flood (GLOF) with flows as great as 10,000 cubic metres a second. Such floods are likely to destroy communication systems and various infrastructures like bridges roads, hydropower projects, foot trails, villages, fields and terraces, and irrigation canals and can cost hundreds or even thousands of lives. Such floods also transport huge amounts of sediment.

In the past two decades, GLOF has become a topic of intense discussion within the development community in Nepal. Studies of the glaciers and glacier lakes were carried out in 1988 by a joint Sino-Nepalese team. In the Arun-Koshi river basin, there are 737 glaciers and 229 glacier lakes in Tibet. Of the glacier lakes, 24 are potentially dangerous. Similarly, there are 45 glacier lakes in the Sun-Koshi basin, out of which 10 are potentially dangerous.

The Dig Tsho GLOF on 4 August, 1985 completely destroyed the nearly completed Namche hydropower plant and all the bridges, trails, cultivation fields, houses and livestock along its path to the confluence of the Dudh-Koshi and the Sun-Koshi rivers at a distance of 90 km (56 mi) from the Dig Tsho glacier. The Dig Tsho glacier is on the terminus of the Langmoche glacier. This event brought into focus the seriousness of such events and the studies to assess the glaciers, glacier lakes and GLOF followed.

According to a Sino-Nepalese study, since the 1940s, there have been at least 10 cases of glacier lake outbursts within the basins investigated. Among these bursts, five occurred in the three glacier lakes of the Arun river basin, and four in the three glacier lakes of the Sun Koshi river basin.

Sapta Koshi High Multipurpose Project (Indo-Nepal)

The governments of India and Nepal have agreed to conduct joint investigations and other studies for the preparation of a detailed project report of the Sapta Koshi High Dam Multipurpose Project and the Sun Koshi Storage-cum-Diversion Scheme to meet the objectives of both the countries for development of hydropower generation, irrigation, flood control and management and navigation.

Envisaged are a 269-metre (883 ft) high concrete or rock-filled dam on the Sapta Koshi river with a dam toe underground power house, with an installed capacity of 3000 MW at 50 percent load factor, a barrage on Sapta Koshi about 8 km (5.0 mi) downstream of the Sapta Koshi High Dam to re-regulate the water being released from the dam with two canals, Eastern Chhatra Canal and Western Chhatra Canal, taking off from the either bank on barrage site to provide water for irrigation both in Nepal and India and navigation through Kosi up to Kursela and also in the reservoir of the Sapta Koshi Dam.

The 1953 Dutch Flood Disaster

On Saturday, 31 January, 1953, the Dutch weather service gave out a warning of an approaching northwester storm on the North Sea. On the intervening night of 31

January–1 February, the storm reached the Netherlands and started increasing. The storm then included heavy winds of 150 km/h.

After the flood of 1916 strong dikes were built that gave people a false sense of safety. Besides, due to limited means of communication, storm warnings could not reach many people. Most people did not have television nor telephones, and there were no late night radio broadcasts. So many people remained unaware of the danger ahead.

The storms caused a change in the water level. The expected ebb tide stayed out and the spring tide was reached somewhere in the middle of the night. At 2 a.m. the Netherlands started flooding, causing dikes to break through at more than 60 locations in three provinces. The southern islands were almost completely flooded, causing thousands of houses and farms to be ruined or dragged into sea. People were fleeing to higher places, such as dikes and attics and were trapped there. On February 1, 1953, the flood increased and water levels were even higher than the previous night. The floods caused a total of 1835 deaths. In some villages up to 10% of the population was killed. More than 47,000 cows and pigs and more than 140.000 pieces of poultry drowned during the flood. A total of more than 200,000 hectares was flooded and 72,000 people were evacuated from their homes. The 1953 flood became the largest natural disaster since the 1570 flood.

Immediately after the flood, the disaster measures were taken to rebuild the dikes. On 18 February, 1953 the Delta Committee was established and in 1955 the Delta law was presented. Starting in 1958, the Delta works were finished in 1986 with the grand opening of the Oosterschelde flood barrier. The Netherlands now has strong dikes and dams that tie together the islands. The flood warning system is improved and the country gained a reputation for its high level of flood protection.

Despite the high level of protection, floods still occur in the Netherlands. In 1993, 1995 and 1998, flooding of the rivers Rhine and Muse caused considerable damage. In 1995, up to 250,000 people were evacuated from their homes. Additionally, global warming may cause a rise in sea level , resulting in more flooding of the country in the future particularly because the height of the western part of the country is slowly decreasing. This means that continual strict water management is required.

Some of the worlds famous floods are as under.

Flood in China

China has always been victim to severe and frequent floods. In 1887 the worst flood occurred in history of China. The dykes were built on both sides of the Yellow River locally known as Huanghe, to prevent river from overflowing and to protect the farmlands in its surroundings. However, from time to time heavy rains have caused the water to overflow the dykes and flood the neighboring farm lands. This is exactly what happened in the flood of 1887. The water from yellow river overtopped its dykes. Many cities and hundred of villages were destroyed. More than 2 million people lost their homes and almost 900,000 people were killed. Yellow river is also called River of Sorrow and it is very understandable.

Huang He (Yellow) River, China 1931

The Huang He River is prone to flooding because of the broad expanse of plain that lies around it. One of the major reasons for the flooding is the high silt content that gives the river its yellow tint (and thus its name). The silt—which constitutes as much as 60% of its volume—builds up until the river actually is higher than the surrounding land. The tendency to flood is exacerbated by ice dams which block the river in Mongolia; the dams back up the water, and then release devastating walls of water when they break.

The history of flooding has prompted the Communist Chinese government to embark on a program of building dams for flood control. The dams, however, have not proven entirely effective and have been the target of criticism from environmentalists.

Huang He (Yellow) River, China 1642

Chinese rebels destroy the dykes along the city of Kaifeng, flooding the surrounding countryside. Death Toll: 300,000.

Yangtze River, China 1931

Although the Huang He has caused more deaths, the Yangtze has had more than 1,000 recorded floods. Death Toll: 145,000.

Huang He (Yellow) River, China 1938

The 1938 flood of the Huang He was caused by Nationalist Chinese troops under Chiang Kai-Shek when they broke the levees in an attempt to turn back advancing Japanese troops. The strategy was partly successful. By 1940, the Japanese were essentially in a stalemate with Chinese forces. Death Toll: 500,000 - 900,000.

Ru River, Banqiao Dam, China 1975

This flood was caused by the collapse of the Banquia Dam, along with several others, following a heavy rain caused by a typhoon. It is the worst dam related collapse in history. Death Toll: 230,000.

Johnstown Flood

The Johnstown flood is also known as Great Flood of 1889. The flood was caused due to heavy rain falls and the failure of the South Fork Dam, which was situated at the upstream of Johnstown, Pennsylvania, USA. The flood resulted in death of 2,200 people and the damage of property worth US$ 17 million. It was the first major disaster for which Red Cross handled relief effort and provided services.

Mississippi Flood of 1927

The Great Mississippi Flood of 1927 was the most destructive river flood in the history of the United States. The flood started with heavy rains in the central plain of Mississippi during summer in 1926. On the day of New Year 1927, the levees at Nashville were already being topped by Cumberland River at (17 m).

On 15th April, 1927, the heavy rain continued for 18 hours and caused flood which overtook the levees and caused the Mounds Landing to break with a volume of water greater than Niagara Falls, Mississippi River also broke out of its levee system.

The water flooded a great amount of area. Many states were affected by this flood. Almost 313 people lost their lives, 700,000 people lost their homes and $285 million of property was lost and damaged as a result of this disaster.

By September, the Mississippi's tributaries in Kansas and Iowa were swollen to capacity. On Christmas Day of 1926, the Cumberland River at Nashville topped levees at 56.2 feet (17 m), a level that remains a record to this day, even exceeding the devastating 2010 floods. Flooding overtook the levees causing the Mounds Landing to break with more than double the water volume of Niagara Falls. The Mississippi River broke out of its levee system in 145 places and flooded 27,000 square miles (70,000 km^2). This water flooded an area 80 km (50 mi) wide and more than 160 km (99 mi) long. The area was inundated up to a depth of 30 feet (10 m). The flood caused over $400 million in damages and killed 246 people in seven states. The flood affected Arkansas, Illinois, Kentucky, Louisiana, Mississippi, Missouri, Tennessee, Texas, Oklahoma and Kansas. Arkansas was hardest hit, with 14% of its territory covered by floodwaters. By May 1927, the Mississippi River below Memphis, Tennessee, reached a width of 60 miles (97 km).

Flood in Thailand

More than 3.4 million people are still affected by Thailand's worst flooding in more than five decades. Many communities across the country have been isolated for weeks, relying on local authorities and organizations like the Thai Red Cross for basic assistance. The situation is particularly difficult for the country's migrant workers....

On a good day it takes about 45 minutes to reach Bangkruai from central Bangkok. Although part of Nonthaburi province, the area is for all intents and purposes. Communities across Bangkok are bracing for the arrival of flood waters, with more than a billion cubic metres of water set to flow through or close to the city.

Almost 2.3 million people have been affected as nearly four months of heavy flooding has washed its way down from Thailand's Northern provinces.

Mississippi Valley, USA, 1937

In the January-February, 1937, approximately 156 trillion tons of water poured down and flooded American Midwest. By January 24, which is also remembered as a Black day, there were overflowing rivers in 12 states. According to the figures more than 250 people drowned and 900 later died due to sickness and injuries. 75,000 homes were destroyed and more than 12,000 miles of land were covered in water.

Flood in Bangladesh

In 1974, just three years after its independence Bangladesh was forced to face of the worst natural disaster in their history and it affected their economy greatly. The monsoons flooded large part of its land. The damage of properties exceeded $2 billion and lives of more that 2,500 people were perished. Soon after diseases like cholera broke out. The quick action of United Nations, millions of worth food and medical supplies were flown in the country and services were provided to rehabilitate those who lost their homes.

Flood in Brazil

In between March and April, 1974, the rains caused flood that resulted in the death of 1,500 people within two weeks. One fifth of the country felt its affects.

The snakes, scorpions and other insects climbed up to the upper houses to flee the rising water. Later meteorologists explained that it was due to the elimination of forests. Lack of trees increases the reflectivity of land hence sending more heat to the atmosphere as a result clouds form violent storms and showers.

Major floods of the world

Flooding occurs all over the world. The examples of major floods mentioned below illustrate this.

- In November 2006, major floods hit large parts of Somalia, killing at least 52 people and displacing 50,000 others. The government appealed for international help to prevent a humanitarian catastrophe

- In November 2006, heavy rain caused large parts of Afghanistan to flood. The official death toll was set on 80, and it took more than two days to reach some of the most severely flooded villages
- In August 2006, a major part of Ethiopia was flooded - Widespread flood of the Mid-Atlantic region of the eastern United States in 2006. At least 16 deaths. Delaware, Columbia, New Jersey, Maryland, Pennsylvania, Virginia, and New York are stricken.
- In May 2006, a major part of Korea was flooded
- In April 2006, the Danube River flooded large parts of Budapest, Hungary. Margit Island was completely under water for a significant amount of time
- In November 2005, some Indian states in the Bay of Bengal were isolated due to heavy rainfall
- In August 2005, major parts of Eastern Europe were flooded due to heavy rainfall
- In August 2005, hurricane Katrina hit New Orleans, the hurricane destroyed levees and floodwalls in the river area, causing 80% of the town to be flooded. Some parts were more than six metres under water. More than 80% of the residents were evacuated, and many were housed in the Louisiana Superdome last-minute. The official death toll from the flood was set on 1,577. Economic and political damage lasted well into 2006
- In July 2005, parts of Mumbai were severely flooded. In some areas the water was more than 4.5 metres high. The flood cost over 700 lives
- In June 2005, Alberta, Canada was flooded, lasting three weeks and demanding 72 lives
- In 2000 large parts of Mozambique were flooded after a cyclone, killing thousands of people

- In the summer of 1998, China experienced major floods of the Yangtze River, killing more than 3,000 people, and leaving 14 million homeless
- In 1994 and 1995 heavy rainfall caused Rivers to flood parts of The Netherlands. Many people in the province of Limburg were evacuated, and dykes in other provinces threatened to break through
- In 1993 the Great Flood hit the American Midwest. The official death toll was 28, and 10,000 homes were destroyed along with 15 million acres of farmland
- In January 1992 large parts of South America flooded
- In 1965 hurricane Betsy flooded major parts of New Orleans, killing 40 people
- In 1957 about 400 people were killed in Louisiana by flooding caused by hurricane Audrey
- In 1955 the Australian Hunter Valley was flooded due to heavy rainfall. In total 25 people were killed, 2,000 cattle drowned, and millions of dollars of crop were destroyed
- In 1953 many Dutch and British citizens were killed in the North Sea flood.
- In 1952 a flood of Lynmouth, England, killed 34 people and destroyed over 80 buildings
- In 1951 heavy rains caused a flood in the Kansas River area, which cost 28 lives. Large parts of Kansas flooded, and damages amounted up to almost one billion dollars
- In 1937 the Ohio River flooded, damaging Pittsburgh and Cairo, Illinois. Approximately 385 people died and about one million were left homeless

- In 1931 major parts of China flooded, causing between 800,000 and 4,000,000 casualties

Besides the floods mentioned above, marked as historical events, there were many more. Some floods are purely mythological. Myths of many different peoples tell of the Great Flood caused by the gods to create a new human race out of a single family.

Chapter – 6

The Great Fires

Fire is a good servant but a bad master, and it has an incredible power to wipe out anything that comes in its way. Fire is one of the important elements of the nature and it helps in the destruction and regeneration of natural objects and resources. Due to its magnificent power to destroy and regenerate, many religions in the earlier times considered fire to be one of the channels through which one can communicate with God. There are many symbols and markings from various religions which tell us how people in the ancient period handled and controlled fire while praying and while attending various religious activities. Hindus believe that fire has a healing property and therefore in their religious functions a Yagna is performed that includes the use of fire. There were several religions in Israel in the earlier times that considered fire to be holy. Similarly, there were many other Indo-European religions that had the same ideas about fire. For example, the followers of Zoroastrianism considered fire a symbol of purity and righteousness and truth.

However, fire has to be handled with a lot of care and attention because it can really change its role and can become life threatening. There are various ways in which fire can become a messenger of death, striking within a fraction of a second killing thousands of people instantly. Natural calamities like earthquakes and volcanoes often lead to fires which strike cities and engulf everything that comes in their way. Bombs and other arms and explosives are also manufactured in a way that their blast causes fires which would burn and kill the bombing target within a matter of seconds. Though today we have the most sophisticated technology and techniques that help us handle and combat various fire situations, let us have a sneak peek into some of the greatest fires in human history.

Great Fire of London

The Great Fire of London was a major conflagration that swept through the central parts of the English city of London, from September 2, to September 5, 1666. The Great Fire started at the bakery of Thomas Farriner on Pudding Lane, shortly after midnight on September 2, and it spread rapidly west across the City of London.

The personal experiences of many Londoners during the fire are glimpsed in letters and memoirs. The two most famous diarists of the Restoration, Samuel Pepys (1633–1703) and John Evelyn (1620–1706), recorded the events and their own reactions day by day, and made great efforts to keep themselves informed of what was happening all over the City and beyond. For example, they both travelled out to the Moorfields park area north of the City on the Wednesday—the fourth day—to view the mighty encampment of distressed refugees there, which shocked them. Their diaries are the most important sources for all modern retellings of the disaster. The most recent books on the fire, by Tinniswood (2003) and Hanson (2001), also rely on the brief memoirs of William Taswell (1651–82), who was a fourteen-year-old schoolboy at Westminster School in 1666.

After two rainy summers in 1664 and 1665, London had lain under an exceptional drought since November 1665, and the wooden buildings were tinder-dry after the long hot summer of 1666. The bakery fire in Pudding Lane spread at first due west, fanned by an eastern gale. The fire gutted the medieval City of London inside the old Roman City Wall. It threatened but did not reach the aristocratic district of Westminster, Charles II's Palace of Whitehall and most of the suburban slums. It consumed 13,200 houses, 87 parish churches, St. Paul's Cathedral, and most of the buildings of the City authorities. It is estimated that it destroyed the homes of 70,000 of the City's 80,000 inhabitants. The death toll from the fire is unknown and is traditionally thought to have been small, as only six verified deaths were recorded. However, this figure has recently been challenged on the grounds that the deaths of poor and middle-class people were not recorded anywhere, and that the heat of the fire may have cremated many victims, leaving no recognisable remains.

The use of the major firefighting technique of the time, the creation of firebreaks by means of demolition, was critically delayed owing to the indecisiveness of the Lord Mayor of London, Sir Thomas Bloodworth. By the time large-scale demolitions were ordered, the wind had already fanned the bakery fire into a firestorm which defeated such measures. On September 3, the fire pushed north into the heart of the City. Order in the streets broke down as rumors' arose of suspicious foreigners setting fires. The fears of the homeless focused on the French and Dutch,

England's enemies in the ongoing Second Anglo-Dutch War; these substantial immigrant groups became victims of lynchings and street violence. On the third day of fire, it spread over most of the City, destroying St. Paul's Cathedral and leaping the River Fleet to threaten Charles II's court at Whitehall, while coordinated firefighting efforts were being mobilised. The battle to quench the fire is considered to have been won by two factors. First, the strong east winds had died down, and, second, the Tower of London garrison used gunpowder to create effective firebreaks to halt the eastward spread of fire.

The social and economic problems created by the disaster were overwhelming. Evacuation from London and resettlement elsewhere were strongly encouraged by Charles II, who feared a rebellion by the dispossessed refugees. Despite numerous radical proposals, London was reconstructed on essentially the same street plan that existed before the fire.

London in the 1660s

By the 1660s, London was by far the largest city in Britain, estimated at half a million inhabitants, which was more than the next fifty towns in England combined. Comparing London to the Baroque magnificence of Paris, John Evelyn called it a "wooden, northern, and inartificial congestion of houses," and expressed alarm about the fire hazard posed by the wood and about the congestion. By "inartificial", Evelyn meant unplanned and makeshift, the result of organic growth and unregulated urban sprawl. A Roman settlement for four centuries, London had become progressively more overcrowded inside its defensive City wall. It had also pushed outwards beyond the wall into squalid extramural slums such as Shoreditch, Holborn, and Southwark and had reached far enough to include the independent City of Westminster.

By the late 17th century, the City proper—the area bounded by the City wall and the Thames river —was only a part of London, covering some 700 acres and home to about 80,000 people, or one-sixth of London's inhabitants. The City was surrounded by a ring of inner suburbs, where most Londoners lived. The City was then as now the commercial heart of the capital, and was the largest market and busiest port in England, dominated by the trading and manufacturing classes. The aristocracy shunned the City and lived either in the countryside beyond the slum suburbs, or in the exclusive Westminster district (the modern West End), the site of Charles II's court at Whitehall. Wealthy people preferred to live at a convenient distance from the traffic-clogged, polluted, unhealthy City, especially after it was hit by a devastating outbreak of bubonic plague in the Plague Year of 1665.

Failures in Fighting the Great Fire

The London Bridge, the only physical connection between the City and the south side of the Thames river, was itself covered with houses and had been noted as a deathtrap in the fire of 1632. By dawn on September 2, 1666, the first day of the Great Fire, these houses were burning, and Samuel Pepys, observing the conflagration from the Tower of London, recorded great concern for friends living on the bridge. There were fears that the flames would cross the London Bridge to threaten the borough of Southwark on the south bank, but this danger was averted by an open space between buildings on the bridge which acted as a firebreak. The 18-foot (5.5 m) high Roman wall enclosing the City put the fleeing homeless at risk of being shut into the inferno. Once the river front was on fire and the escape route by boat cut off, the only exits were the eight gates in the wall. During the first couple of days, few people had any notion of fleeing the burning City altogether. They would simply remove what they could carry of their belongings to the nearest 'safe house', in many cases the parish church, or the precincts of St. Paul's Cathedral, only to have to move again hours later. Some moved their belongings and themselves 'four and five times' in a single day. The perception of a need to get beyond the walls only took root late on September 3, and then there were near-panic scenes at the narrow gates as distraught refugees tried to get out with their bundles, carts, horses and wagons.

The crucial factor which frustrated firefighting efforts was the narrowness of the streets. Even under normal circumstances, the mix of carts, wagons and pedestrians in the undersized alleys was subject to frequent traffic jams and gridlock. During the fire, the passages were additionally blocked by refugees camping in them with their rescued belongings, or escaping outwards, away from the centre of destruction, as demolition teams and fire engine crews struggled in vain to move in towards it.

The use of water to extinguish the fire was also frustrated. In principle, water was available from a system of elm pipes which supplied 30,000 houses via a high water tower at Cornhill, filled from the river at high tide, and also via a reservoir of Hertfordshire spring water in Islington. It was often possible to open a pipe near a burning building and connect it to a hose to play on a fire, or fill buckets. Further, Pudding Lane was close to the river. Theoretically, all the lanes from the river up to the bakery and adjoining buildings should have been manned with double rows of firefighters passing full buckets up to the fire and empty buckets back down to the river. This did not happen, or at least was no longer happening by the time Pepys viewed the fire from the river at mid-morning on Sunday. Pepys comments in his diary that nobody was trying to put it out, but instead they fled from it in fear, hurrying "to remove their goods, and leave all to the fire." The flames crept towards the river front with little interference from the overwhelmed community and soon torched the flammable warehouses along the wharves. The resulting conflagration not only cut off the firefighters from the immediate water supply from the river but also set alight the water wheels under the London Bridge which pumped water to the Cornhill water tower; the direct access to the river and the supply of piped water failed together.

Deaths and Destruction

The Londoners Lamentation, a broadside ballad published in 1666, gave an account of the fire, and of the limits of its destruction.

Only a few deaths from the fire are officially recorded, and deaths are traditionally believed to have been few. Porter gives the figure as eight and Tinniswood as "in single figures", although he adds that some deaths must have gone unrecorded and that, besides direct deaths from burning and smoke inhalation, refugees also perished in the impromptu camps. Hanson contests the idea that there were only a few deaths, enumerating known deaths from hunger and exposure among survivors of the holocaust "huddled in shacks or living among the ruins that had once been their homes" in the cold winter that followed, including, for instance, the dramatist James Shirley and his wife.

The fire, fed not merely by wood, fabrics, and thatch, but also by the oil, pitch, coal, tallow, fats, sugar, alcohol, turpentine, and gunpowder stored in the riverside district, melted the imported steel lying along the wharves [melting point between 1,250 C (2,300 F) and 1,480 C (2,700 F)] and the great iron chains and locks on the City gates [melting point between 1,100 C (2,000 F) and 1,650 C (3000 F)]. Nor would anonymous bone fragments have been of much interest to the hungry people sifting through the tens of thousands of tons of rubble and debris after the fire, looking for valuables, or to the workmen clearing away the rubble later during the rebuilding.

The material destruction has been computed at 13,500 houses, 87 parish churches, 44 Company Halls, the Royal Exchange, the Custom House, St. Paul's Cathedral, the Bridewell Palace and other City prisons, the General Letter Office, and the three western city gates, Ludgate, Newgate, and Aldersgate. The monetary value of the loss, first estimated at £100,000,000 in the currency of the time, was later reduced to an uncertain £10,000,000 (over £1 billion in 2005 pounds). Evelyn believed that he saw as many as "200,000 people of all ranks and stations dispersed, and lying along their heaps of what they could save" in the fields towards Islington and Highgate.

Aftermath

An example of the urge to identify scapegoats for the fire is the acceptance of the confession of a simple-minded French watchmaker, Robert Hubert, who claimed he was an agent of the Pope and had started the Great Fire in Westminster. He later changed his story to say that he had started the fire at the bakery in Pudding Lane. Hubert was convicted, despite some misgivings about his fitness to plead, and hanged at Tyburn on September 28, 1666. After his death, it became apparent that he had not arrived in London until two days after the fire started. These allegations that Catholics had started the fire were exploited as powerful political propaganda by opponents of pro-Catholic Charles II's court, mostly during the Popish Plot and the exclusion crisis later in his reign.

Abroad in the Netherlands, the Great Fire of London was seen as a divine retribution for Holmes's Bonfire, the burning by the English of a Dutch town during the Second Anglo-Dutch War.

In the chaos and unrest after the fire, Charles II feared another London rebellion. He encouraged the homeless to move away from London and settle elsewhere, immediately issuing a proclamation that "all Cities and Towns whatsoever shall without any contradiction receive the said distressed persons and permit them the free exercise of their manual trades." A special Fire Court was set up to deal with disputes between tenants and landlords and decide who should rebuild, based on one's ability to pay. The Court was in session from February 1667 to September 1672. Cases were heard and a verdict usually given within a day, and without the Fire Court, lengthy legal wrangles would have seriously delayed the rebuilding which was so necessary if London was to recover.

Encouraged by Charles, radical rebuilding schemes for the gutted City poured in. If it had been rebuilt under some of these plans, London would have rivalled Paris in Baroque magnificence. The Crown and the City authorities attempted to establish "to whom all the houses and ground did in truth belong" in order to negotiate with their owners about compensation for the large-scale remodelling that these plans entailed, but that unrealistic idea had to be abandoned. Exhortations to bring workmen and measure the plots on which the houses had stood were mostly ignored by people worried about day-to-day survival as well as by those who had left the capital. With the shortage of labour following the fire, it was impossible to secure workmen for the purpose. Apart from Wren and Evelyn, it is known that Robert Hooke, Valentine Knight and Richard Newcourt proposed rebuilding plans.

With the complexities of ownership unresolved, none of the grand Baroque schemes for a City of piazzas and avenues could be realised; there was nobody to negotiate with, and no means of calculating how much compensation should be paid. Instead, much of the old street plan was recreated in the new City, with improvements in hygiene and fire safety: wider streets, open and accessible wharves along the length of the Thames, with no houses obstructing access to the river, and, most importantly, buildings constructed of brick and stone, not wood. New public buildings were created on their predecessors' sites; perhaps the most famous is St. Paul's Cathedral and its smaller cousins, Christopher Wren's 50 new churches.

On Charles' initiative, a Monument to the Great Fire of London, designed by Christopher Wren and Robert Hooke, was erected near Pudding Lane. Standing 61 metres tall and known simply as "The Monument", it is a familiar London landmark which has given its name to a tube station. In 1668, accusations against the Catholics were added to the inscription on The Monument which read, in part:

"Here by permission of heaven, hell broke loose upon this Protestant city... the most dreadful Burning of this City; begun and carried on by the treachery and malice of the Popish faction... Popish frenzy which wrought such horrors, is not yet quenched..."

Aside from the four years of James II's rule from 1685 to 1689, the inscription remained in place until 1830 and the passage of the Catholic Emancipation Act.

Another monument, the Golden Boy of Pye Corner in Smithfield, marks the spot where the fire stopped. According to the inscription, the fact that the fire started at Pudding Lane and stopped at Pye Corner was an indication that the Fire was evidence of God's wrath on the City of London for the sin of gluttony.

The Great Plague epidemic of 1665 is believed to have killed a sixth of London's inhabitants, or 80,000 people, and it is sometimes suggested, as plague epidemics did not recur in London after the fire, that the fire saved lives in the long run by burning down so much unsanitary housing with their rats and their fleas which transmitted the plague. Historians disagree as to whether the fire played a part in preventing subsequent major outbreaks. The Museum of London website claims that there was a connection, while historian Roy Porter points out that the fire left the most insalubrious parts of London, the slum suburbs, untouched. Alternative epidemiological explanations have been put forward along with the observation that the disease disappeared from almost every other European city around the same time.

Following the Great Fire, the thoroughfares of Queen Street and King Street were newly laid out, cutting across more ancient thoroughfares in the City, creating a new route up from the Thames to the Guildhall; they were the only notable new streets following the fire's destruction of much of the City.

Chicago Fire

The Chicago Fire was a conflagration that burned from Sunday, October 8, to early Tuesday, October 10, 1871, killing hundreds and destroying about 4 square miles (10 km^2) in Chicago, Illinois. Though the fire was one of the largest US disasters of the 19th century, the rebuilding that began almost immediately spurred Chicago's development into one of the most populous and economically important American cities.

Origin

The fire started at about 9 p.m. on Sunday, October 8, 1871 in or around a small barn that bordered the alley behind 137 DeKoven Street. The traditional account of the origin of the fire is that it was started by a cow kicking over a lantern in the barn owned by Patrick and Catherine O'Leary. Michael Ahern, the *Chicago Republican* reporter who created the cow story, admitted in 1893 that he had made it up because he thought it would make colourful copy.

The fire's spread was aided by the city's overuse of wood for building, a drought prior to the fire, and strong winds from the southwest that carried flying embers toward the heart of the city. The city also made fatal errors by not reacting soon enough and citizens were apparently unconcerned when it began. The firefighters were also exhausted from fighting a fire that happened the day before. The firefighters fought the fire through the entire day and became extremely exhausted. Eventually the fire jumped to a nearby neighbourhood and began to devastate mansions, houses and apartments. Almost everything that crossed the fire's path was made of wood that had been dried out for quite a while. After two days of the city burning down, it began to rain and doused the remaining fire. It is said that over 300 people died in the fire and over 100,000 were left homeless.

After the Fire

Once the fire had ended, the smoldering remains were still too hot for a survey of the damage to be completed for days. Eventually, it was determined that the fire destroyed an area about four miles (6 km) long and averaging 3/4 mile (1 km) wide, encompassing more than 2,000 acres (810 ha). Destroyed were more than 73 miles (120 km) of roads, 120 miles (190 km) of sidewalk, 2,000 lamp-posts, 17,500 buildings, and $222 million in property—about a third of the city's valuation. Of the 300,000 inhabitants, 90,000 were left homeless. Between two and three million books were destroyed from private library collections.

After the fire, 125 bodies were recovered. Final estimates of the fatalities ranged from 200–300, considered a small number for such a large fire. In later years, other disasters would claim many more lives: at least 605 died in the Iroquois Theater Fire in 1903; and, in 1915, 835 died in the sinking of the Eastland excursion boat in the Chicago River. Yet the Great Chicago Fire remains Chicago's most well-known disaster for the magnitude of the destruction and the city's recovery and growth. Almost immediately, reform began in the city's fire standards, spurred by the efforts of leading insurance executives and fire prevention reformers.

Chicago emerged from the fire with one of the country's leading firefighting forces. Land speculators, such as Gurdon Saltonstall Hubbard, and business owners quickly set about rebuilding the city. Donations of money, food, clothing and furnishings arrived quickly from across the nation. The first load of lumber for rebuilding was delivered the day the last burning building was extinguished. Only 22 years later, Chicago hosted more than 21 million visitors during the World's Columbian Exposition. Another example of Chicago's rebirth from the Great Fire ashes is the now famed Palmer House hotel. The original building burned to the ground in the fire just 13 days after its grand opening. Without hesitating, Potter Palmer secured a loan and rebuilt the hotel in a lot across the street from the original, proclaiming it to be "The World's First Fireproof Building".

The city of Singapore, Michigan provided a large portion of the lumber to rebuild Chicago. As a result the town of Singapore was so heavily deforested that the area turned into barren sand dunes and the town had to be abandoned.

Questions about the Origin of Fire

According to *Chicago Tribune,* Catherine O'Leary seemed the perfect scapegoat: she was a woman, an immigrant and Catholic, a combination which did not fare well in the political climate of the time in Chicago. This story was circulating in Chicago even before the flames had died out, and it was noted in the *Chicago Tribune*'s first post-fire issue. Michael Ahern, the reporter who came up with the story, retracted the "cow-and-lantern" story in 1893, admitting it was fabricated. More recently, amateur historian Richard Bales has come to believe the fire started when Daniel "Pegleg" Sullivan, who first reported the fire, ignited hay in the barn while trying to steal milk. However, evidence recently reported in the *Chicago Tribune* by Anthony DeBartolo suggests Louis M. Cohn may have started the fire during a craps game. Cohn may also have admitted to starting the fire in a lost will. Dennis Regan was a resident of Chicago and a neighbour of the O'Learys. It is believed that he was an accomplice of Sullivan in the start of the Great Chicago Fire.

An alternative theory, first suggested in 1882, is that the Great Chicago Fire was caused by a meteor shower. At a 2004 conference of the Aerospace Corporation and the American Institute of Aeronautics and Astronautics, engineer and physicist Robert Wood suggested that the fire began when Biela's Comet broke up over the Midwest and rained down below. That four large fires took place, all on the same day, all on the shores of Lake Michigan suggests a common root cause. Eyewitnesses reported sighting spontaneous ignitions, lack of smoke, "balls of fire" falling from the sky, and blue flames. According to Wood, these accounts suggest that the fires were caused by the methane that is commonly found in comets. However, since meteorites are not known to start fires and are usually cool to the touch after reaching the ground, this theory has not found favour in the scientific community.

Surviving Structures

- St. Michael's Church, Old Town
- Chicago Water Tower
- Chicago Avenue Pumping Station

Related Fires

Three other major fires occurred along the shores of Lake Michigan at the same time as the Great Chicago Fire. Some 250 miles (400 km) to the north, a forest fire driven by strong winds consumed the town of Peshtigo, Wisconsin, along with a dozen other villages, killing 1,200 to 2,500 people and charring approximately 1.5 million acres (6,000 km). Though the Peshtigo Fire remains the deadliest in American history, the remoteness of the region meant it was little noticed at the time. Across the lake to the east, the town of Holland, Michigan, and other nearby areas burned to the ground. Some 100 miles (160 km) to the north of Holland the lumbering community of Manistee, Michigan, also went up in flames in what became known as The Great Michigan Fire. Farther east, along the shore of Lake Huron, the Port Huron Fire swept through Port Huron, Michigan and much of Michigan's "Thumb". Also on October 9, 1871 a fire swept through the City of Urbana, Illinois, 140 miles (230 km) south of Chicago, destroying portions of its downtown area. Windsor, Ontario likewise burned on October 12.

Chapter – 7

Famous Volcanoes

Volcanoes are mountains with a vent from which molten material from deep within the earth can spew under the appropriate conditions. A volcano may be defined in the following way:

1. An opening or vent in the earth's crust through which hot rock molten, rock (lava), ash, steam and gases are ejected.
2. A similar opening on the surface of another planet.
3. A mountain formed by the materials ejected from a volcano.

When pressure from the molten rock beneath the earth's surface becomes too great, the rock, usually accompanied by lava or gases, escapes through a fissure or vent in the crust of the earth. 'Volcano' is the term given to both the vent and the conical mountain left by the overflow of the erupted lava, rock and ash. A mountain or hill, generally steep-sided, is formed by accumulation of magma (molten rock with associated gas and crystals) erupted through openings or volcanic vents in the earth's crust; the term volcano also refers to the vent itself. During the evolution of a long-lived volcano, a permanent shift in the locus of principal vent activity can produce a satellite volcanic accumulation as large as or larger than the parent volcano, in effect forming a new volcano on the flanks of the old. Volcanoes are described as active, dormant, or extinct.

Planetary exploration has revealed dramatic evidence of volcanoes and their products on the earth's moon, Mars, Mercury, Venus, and the moons of Jupiter, Neptune, and Uranus on a scale much more vast than on Earth.

Volcanoes are usually located at the junction of the earth's lithospheric plates. More than 80% of the earth's surface comes from volcanoes. Innumerable volcanic eruptions formed the sea floor and some mountains; gaseous emissions from volcanoes formed the earth's atmosphere.

The name "volcano" is said to have come from Vulcano, a volcanic island in the Aeolian Islands of Italy. The name Vulcano originates from Vulcan, a god of fire in Roman mythology. The study of volcanoes is called volcanology.

Seismographic monitoring, tiltmeters and surveillance by satellite all serve to predict activity in a volcano. Gas and steam emissions can also indicate an impending volcanic eruption.

Volcanoes have existed for geologic eons, but many are no longer active. The number of volcanoes worldwide that earth scientists consider active—those that can erupt—was about 500 in the mid-1990s. More than half of these volcanoes are part of the 'Ring of Fire,' a region that encircles the Pacific Ocean. In the United States most active volcanoes are located in Alaska or in Hawaii, which consists of a group of islands formed by earlier volcanic eruptions. The West Coast of the continental United States also has a relatively inactive volcanic zone.

The two principal volcanoes in the United States are Mauna Loa and Kilauea, both in the Hawaiian island chain. Mauna Loa is the world's largest active volcano. Taller than Mount Everest, Mauna Loa's summit rises 56,000 ft (17,000 m) from its base below sea level. Mauna Loa was last erupted in 1975 and 1984. Kilauea is in almost continual eruption. Alaskan eruptions occurred in 1989, when Mount Redoubt, along Cook Inlet, southwest of Anchorage, erupted; in 1992, when Mount Spurr erupted; and in 1996, when an unnamed volcano on Augustine Island (also in Cook Inlet) erupted. Although not in the United States, Mount Pinatubo in the Philippines projected enough ash into the stratosphere during its eruption in 1991 to have a significant cooling effect on the US climate for several years. Eruptions in the lower 48 states are rare but certainly not unknown: for example, the widely publicised eruption of Mount St. Helens in Washington State in 1980. Despite dire predictions and a minor eruption in 1990, the area surrounding Mount St. Helens had largely recovered from the effects of the 1980 eruption by 2000.

There are two volcanic observatories in the United States. One, established on Kilauea in 1912, is the second oldest in the world, ranking behind only one in Italy, on Mount Vesuvius. Following the eruption of Mount St. Helens in 1980, an observatory was established there.

Types of Volcanic Eruptions

Lava can flow slowly or erupt violently into the air. The rocks blown out of a volcano – called pyroclastic rocks – fall back to the earth as dust, ash, cinder or pumice. Most volcanic ash falls to the ground. Cemented together by water, the volcano ash forms a rock called volcanic tuff.

Depending on how often they erupt, volcanoes may be classified as active, intermittent, dormant, or extinct. Listed below are different types volcanic eruptions:

- **Pyroclastic Flows** — Mixtures of hot gas, ash and other volcanic rocks which travel very quickly down the slope of a volcano. The heat is so great that anyone caught in such a flow will most likely be killed. The speed of the pyroclastic flow is so fast that it cannot be outrun and it is best to evacuate all people living near a volcano that is suspected of producing this kind of flow.
- **Nues Ardentes** — Literally, it means 'incandescent cloud.' One of the most destructive kinds of volcanic eruptions, it occurs when viscous magma erupts under reasonably low pressure, causing a glowing cloud of ash and pumice to be thrown into the air. This mass avalanches back to the earth before it can cool off. Made up of a mixture of gas, lava, blocks, ash and pumice, nues ardentes can reach speeds up to 310 mi/hr (500 km/hr).
- **Volcanic Ash** — It is volcanic rock which is exploded from a vent in fragments less than an inch (2.5 cm) in size. Volcanic ash particles are like small sharp glass particles that damage anything they come across. During heavy rains of ash, buildings may collapse and people and animals may be suffocated.
- **Lahars** — These are mudflows formed by the mixing of volcanic particles and water. The force of a lahar is so great that buildings may be crushed or carried away; those that are left may become partially or completely buried by one or more cement-like layers of rock debris. Since the lahars move so quickly, people caught in their path may drown, be crushed or be asphyxiated. It is best to evacuate people living in the vicinity of a volcano that may produce lahars.
- **Debris Avalanches** — Debris is transported away from the volcano's slope due to the instability of the slope. Debris avalanches usually occur on large, steep

volcanoes, and are one of the most hazardous but least common of volcanic dangers. The bigger the avalanche, the greater its speed and the more dangerous it is.

- **Landslide** — It is a gradual, downslope movement of a mass of bedrock. The mixture of debris from a landslide or avalanche with water may produce harmful lahars.
- Volcanic eruptions can precipitate other natural disasters, such as earthquakes, flash floods, acid rain, fires and tsunamis.

Safety Measures

Anyone living in the vicinity of a volcano should have a disaster supply kit prepared, including a pair of goggles and disposable breathing mask for each member of the family. Of course, it is always advisable to stay away from active volcano sites.

If a volcano erupts, follow the precautions mentioned below:

- If possible, immediately leave the area.
- If caught near a stream, beware of mudflows. They can move faster than you can walk or run. Look upstream before crossing a bridge, and do not cross the bridge if a mudflow is approaching.
- Avoid river valleys and low-lying areas.
- Protect yourself from falling ash by wearing long-sleeved shirts and long pants. Use goggles and wear eyeglasses instead of contact lenses, and wear a dust mask or hold a damp cloth over your face to help with breathing.
- Stay away from areas downwind from the volcano. It is best to stay indoors until the ash has settled unless there is a danger of the roof collapsing. Be sure to close doors, windows, and all ventilation in

the house (chimney vents, furnaces, air conditioners, fans, and other vents).

- When the ash has settled, clear it from roofs and rain gutters.
- Avoid driving, which can stir up volcanic ash that can clog engines, damage moving parts, and stall vehicles. If you have to drive, keep speed down to 35 mi/hr (56 km/hr) or slower.

History's Worst Volcanic Eruptions

Listed below are some of the major volcanic eruptions in the world.

- Crater Lake in Oregon was formed from a high volcano that lost its top after a series of tremendous explosions about 6,600 years ago.
- Mount Vesuvius, in Italy, has erupted several times. The most devastating of the eruptions occurred in AD 79, destroying the cities of Pompeii and Herculaneum.
- Indonesia's Krakatoa has erupted several times, with the last and most devastating eruption in 1883. The resulting tsunami killed more than 36,000 people in the area of Java and Sumatra. New islands were formed by the huge amount of lava and ash and debris scattered as far away as Madagascar. The sound of the explosion was heard as far away as Perth, Australia (nearly 2000 mi/3100 km), and Rodrigues, near Mauritius (approximately 3000 mi/ 4800 km).
- In 1963, Mount Agung in Bali erupted, taking the lives of some 1,100 people.
- On May 18, 1980, after more than 100 years of dormancy, Mount St. Helens erupted in Washington. The rock debris carried by a lateral blast of Mount St. Helens travelled as fast as 250 mi/hr (402 km/hr).

Fifty-eight people were killed and there was a resulting $1.2 billion in damages.

- The 1992 eruption of Mount Pinatubo in the Philippines Islands caused 342 deaths; more than 250,000 people had to be evacuated. Vast amounts of aerosols were spewed into the stratosphere, forming a global layer of sulfuric acid haze that lasted for several months. Global temperatures dropped by about 0.9 degrees F (0.5 C).

Believe it or not, there are advantages of living near a volcano. Volcanoes provide geothermal resources which are converted into energy. This type of energy is very clean and the resources are nearly inexhaustible. Moreover, when a volcano erupts, it throws out a lot of ash. Although initially this ash is very harmful to the environment, in the long run, the ash layer will turn into extremely fertile soil, rich in minerals. The volcanic ash is also a good polishing and cleansing agent. And tourists flock to volcano sites because the sunsets and views that they create can be breathtakingly beautiful.

Distribution of Volcanoes

Most of the 500 active volcanoes, known on the Earth, mostly reside along or near the boundaries of the dozen or so lithospheric plates that compose the earth's solid surface. Lithospheric plates show three distinct types of boundaries: divergent or spreading margins—adjacent plates are pulling apart; convergent margins (subduction zones)—plates are moving toward each other and one is being destroyed; and transform margins—one plate is sliding horizontally past another. All these types of plate motion are well demonstrated in the Circum-Pacific region, that is, the 'Ring of Fire' in which reside many active volcanoes.

Some of the most violent eruptions take place along convergent boundaries where one plate margin is forced beneath another. The most famous such boundary is the 'Ring of Fire' bordering the Pacific Ocean. The island arcs and mountain ranges of this 'Ring of Fire' have seen gigantic explosions, among them the eruptions of Mount Pinatubo in the Philippines in 1991, Mount Saint Helens in the US state of Washington in 1980, and Krakatoa (Krakatau) in Indonesia in 1883.

Continental volcanoes are also associated with converging plate boundaries, such as the volcanoes of the Cascade Range along the west coast of the United States. Isolated volcanoes also form in the mid-ocean area of the Pacific apparently unrelated to crustal plate boundaries. These sea mounts and volcanic island chains, such as the Hawaiian chain, may form from rising magma regions called hot spots; an example of a continental hot spot is found at Yellowstone National Park.

Volcanic activity is also common at divergent boundaries, where two plates slowly pull apart and allow molten rock to escape to the surface. The most prominent example of this volcanic activity is the Mid-Atlantic Ridge, site of volcanic islands such as Iceland, the Azores, Ascension, Saint Helena, and Tristan da Cunha.

Yet another type of volcanic activity is found on the island of Hawaii, located on a "hot spot" near the middle of the Pacific Plate where plumes of partially melted rock rise from below the earth's crust; there the volcanoes Kilauea and Mauna Loa frequently eject streams and fountains of lava. Some of the best-known volcanism takes place around the Mediterranean Sea, where the eruptions of Mount Etna, Vesuvius, the islands of Stromboli and Vulcano, and other volcanoes have been observed for millennia. Some volcanoes have cultural or religious significance for the peoples around them; these include Misti Volcano in Peru, Mount Fuji in Japan, and Ol Doinyo Lengai in Tanzania.

Some volcanoes, however, are not associated with plate boundaries, and many of these so-called intraplate volcanoes form roughly linear chains in the interior parts of the oceanic plates, for example, the Hawaiian-Emperor, Austral, Society, and Line archipelagoes in the Pacific Basin. Intraplate volcanism also has resulted in voluminous outpourings of fluid lava to form extensive plateau basalts, or of more viscous and siliceous pyroclastic products to form ash flow plains.

Cone and Shield Volcanoes

Much of the earth's solid surface, on land and below the sea, has been shaped by volcanic activity. Landscape features of volcanic origin may be either positive (constructional) forms, the result of accumulation of volcanic materials, or negative forms, the result of the lack of accumulation or collapse.

The shape and size of a volcano can vary widely between the simple forms of composite and shield volcanoes, depending on magma viscosity, eruptive style (explosive versus nonexplosive), migration of vent locations, duration and complexity of eruptive history, and post-eruption modifications.

Shapes of volcanoes include composite cones, or stratovolcanoes, with steep concave sides such as Mt. St. Helens in the W United States; shield cones have gentle slopes and can be relatively large such as the Hawaiian Islands; and cinder cones as Pariìcutin in Mexico, with steep slopes made of cinderlike materials.

Cone volcanoes are associated with thick lava and much ash. Not all volcanoes show a graceful, symmetrical cone shape, such as that exemplified by Mount Fuji, Japan. Most volcanoes, especially those near tectonic plate boundaries, are more irregular, though of grossly conical shape. Such volcanoes (stratovolcanoes) typically erupt explosively and are composed dominantly of andesitic, relatively viscous and short lava flows, interlayered with beds of ash and cinder that thin away from the principal vents.

Volcanoes constructed primarily of fluid basaltic lava flows, which may spread great distances from the vents, typically are gentle-sloped, broadly upward convex structures. Such shield volcanoes, classic examples of which are Mauna Loa volcano, Hawaii, tend to form in the oceanic intraplate regions and are associated with hot-spot volcanism. Shield volcanoes are formed when less thick lava wells up and spreads over a large area, creating a wide, gently sloping landform. Explosive eruptions build up steep-sided cones, while the nonexplosive ones usually form broad, low lava cones.

Cones range in height from a few feet to nearly 30,000 ft (9 km) above their base. Usually the cone has as its apex a cavity, or crater, which contains the mouth of the vent. Such craters are typically less than 1 mi (1.6 km) across, but larger craters, called calderas, ranging in diameter from 3 mi to—in a few instances—50 mi (5-80 km), are formed by particularly large eruptions.

Some of the largest volcanic edifices are not shaped like the composite or shield volcanoes. In certain regions of the world, voluminous extrusions of very fluid basaltic lava from dispersed fissure swarms have built broad, nearly flat-topped accumulations. These voluminous outpourings of lava are known as flood basalts or plateau basalts

Volcanic Vents

Volcanic vents, channelways for magma to ascend toward the surface, can be grouped into two general types: fissure and central (pipelike). Magma consolidating below the surface in fissures or pipes forms a variety of igneous bodies, but magma breaking the surface produces fissure or pipe eruptions. Fissures, most of them less than 10 ft

(3 m) wide, may form in the summit region of a volcano, on its flanks, or near its base; central vents tend to be restricted to the summit area of a volcano. For some volcanoes or volcanic regions, swarms of fissure vents are clustered in swaths called rift zones.

Volcanic Products

Magma erupted onto the Earth's surface is called lava. If the lava is chilled and solidifies quickly, it forms volcanic glass; slower rates of chilling result in greater crystallization before complete solidification. Lava may accrete near the vent to form various minor structures or may pour out in streams called lava flows, which may travel many tens of miles from the vents. During more violent eruption, lava torn into fragments and hurled into the air. This lava is called pyroclastic (fire-broken materials).

Volcanic Gases

Violent volcanic explosions may throw dust and aerosols high into the stratosphere from where they may drift across the surface of the globe for many thousands of miles. Most of the solid particles in the volcanic cloud settle out within a few days, and nearly all settle out within a few weeks, but the gaseous aerosols (principally sulfuric acid droplets) may remain suspended in the stratosphere for several years. Such stratospheric clouds of volcanic aerosols, if sufficiently voluminous and long-lived, can have an impact on global climate. In general, water vapour is the most abundant constituent in volcanic gases; the water is mostly of meteoric (atmospheric) origin, but in some volcanoes can have a significant magmatic or juvenile component. Excluding water vapour, the most abundant gases are the various species of carbon, sulfur, hydrogen, chlorine, and fluorine. Mudflows are common on steep-side volcanoes where poorly indurated or nonwelded pyroclastic material is abundant. Probably by far the most common cause of mudflows is simply heavy rain saturating a thick cover of loose, unstable pyroclastic material on the steep slope of the volcano, transforming the material into a mobile, water-saturated "mud," which can rush downslope at a speed as great as 50–55 mi (80–90 km) per hour. Such a dense, fast-moving mass can be highly destructive, sweeping up everything loose in its path.

Submarine Volcanism

Deep submarine volcanism occurs along the spreading ridges that zigzag for thousands of miles across the ocean floor. These ridges are exposed above sea level only in Iceland. Because of the logistical difficulties in making direct observations posed by the great ocean depths, no deep submarine volcanic activity has been actually observed during eruption. However, evidence that deep-sea eruptions are happening is clearly indicated by (a) seismic and acoustic monitoring networks; (b) the presence of deep-ocean floor hydrothermal vents; (c) episodic hydrothermal discharges, measured and mapped as thermal and geochemical anomalies in the ocean water; and (d) the detection of new lava flows in certain segments of the oceanic ridge system. Volcanic eruptions in shallow water are very similar in character to those on land but, on average, are probably somewhat more explosive, owing to heating of water and resultant violent generation of supercritical steam. Much of the ocean basin appears to be floored by basaltic lava.

Fumaroles and Hot Springs

Vents at which volcanic gases issue without lava or after the eruption are known as fumaroles. They are found on active volcanoes during and between eruptions and on dormant volcanoes, persisting long after the volcano itself has become inactive. Fumaroles grade into hot springs and geysers. The water of most, if not all, hot springs is predominantly of meteoric origin, and is not water liberated from magma. Some hot springs are of volcanic origin and the water may contain volcanic gases.

Distribution of Volcanoes

Over 500 active volcanoes are known on the Earth, mostly along or near the boundaries of the dozen or so lithospheric plates that compose the Earth's solid surface. Lithospheric plates show three distinct types of boundaries: divergent or spreading margins—adjacent plates are pulling apart; convergent margins (subduction zones)—plates are moving toward each other and one is being destroyed; and transform margins—one plate is sliding horizontally past another. All these types of plate motion are well demonstrated in the Circum-Pacific region, in which many active volcanoes form the so-called Ring of Fire. Some volcanoes, however, are not associated with plate boundaries, and many of these so-called intraplate volcanoes form roughly linear chains in the interior parts of the oceanic plates, for example, the Hawaiian-Emperor, Austral, Society, and Line archipelagoes in the Pacific Basin. Intraplate volcanism also has resulted in voluminous outpourings of fluid lava to form extensive plateau basalts, or of more viscous and siliceous pyroclastic products to form ash flow plains.

Volcanic Eruptions

More than 500 volcanoes are known to have erupted on the earth's surface since historic times, and many more have erupted on the ocean floor unobserved by humans. Fifty volcanoes have erupted in the United States, which ranks third, behind Indonesia and Japan, in the number of historically active volcanoes. Of the world's active volcanoes, more than half are found in Ring of Fire around the perimeter of the Pacific, about a third on mid-oceanic islands and in an arc along the south of the Indonesian islands, and about a tenth in the Mediterranean area, Africa, and Asia Minor.

Evidence of extraterrestrial volcanic activity also has been found. Space probes have detected the remnants of ancient eruptions on earth's moon, Mars (which has the largest volcano in the solar system, Olympus Mons, 340 mi/550 km across and 15 mi/24 km high), and Mercury; these probably originated billions of years ago, since these bodies are no longer capable of volcanic activity. Triton (a satellite of Neptune), Io (a satellite of Jupiter), and Venus are known to be volcanically active. The volcanic processes that occur in the outer portion of the solar system are very different from those in the inner part. Eruptions on the earth, Venus, Mercury, and Mars are of rocky material and are driven by internal heat. Io's eruptions are probably sulfur or sulfur compounds driven by tidal interactions with Jupiter. Triton's eruptions are of very volatile compounds, such as methane or nitrogen, driven by seasonal heating from the sun.

Terrestrial volcanic eruptions may take one or more of four chief forms, or phases, known as Hawaiian, Strombolian, Vulcanian, and Peleean. In the Hawaiian phase, there is a relatively quiet effusion of basaltic lava unaccompanied by explosions or the ejection of fragments; the eruptions of Mauna Loa on the island of Hawaii are typical. The Strombolian phase derives its name from the volcano Stromboli in the Lipari, or Aeolian, Islands, north of Sicily. It applies to continuous but mild discharges in which viscous lava is emitted in recurring explosions; the ejection of incandescent material produces luminous clouds. A more explosive volcanic eruption is the Vulcanian, where the magma (lava before emission) accumulates in the upper level of the vent but is blocked by a hardened plug of lava that forms between consecutive explosions. When the explosive gases have reached a critical pressure within the volcano, masses of solid and liquid rock erupt into the air and clouds of vapour form over the crater. The Peleean, derived from Mt. Pelée, is the most violent, emitting fine ash; hot, gas-charged fragments of lava; and superheated steam in an incandescent "cloud" that travels downhill at great speed. Eruptions are often accompanied by torrential rains caused by the condensation of steam. The erupted fragments vary in size, including minute particles of volcanic dust and ash, lapilli (cinders or pellets), bombs (rounded or ellipsoidal masses of hardened magma), and huge masses called blocks. Minute dust and ash and aerosols carried high into the earth's atmosphere can have a cooling effect on the climate; the dust and ash can also be a hazard to air travel. The 1783 eruption of Laki, S Iceland, had devastating effects on local livestock and, as result, the populace; the resulting sulfur dioxide haze that spread over parts of Europe is believed to have negatively affected the health of the inhabitants.

Mount Vesuvius

Mt. Vesuvius, the active volcano that looms over the Bay of Naples in southern Italy, has erupted well over 30 times that we know of. And yet its most famous eruption took place way back in A.D. 79, when a multiday eruption of lava and ash covered the cities of Pompeii and Stabiae in ash. Pliny the Younger, author of the only surviving eyewitness account, described a sudden explosion followed by blankets of ash that fell on people as they tried to escape. The total number of Vesuvius' victims will most likely never be known, but archeologists are aware of at least 1,000.

Krakatoa

In 1883, the volcano on the Indonesian island of Krakatoa erupted with 13,000 times the power of an atomic bomb. The sound of the spewing smoke and rock was reportedly heard thousands of miles away, as far as islands off the eastern coast of Africa. Hundreds in a nearby Sumatran town died almost instantly when flaming ash incinerated their homes, and many more were washed away by subsequent megatsunamis. An estimated 36,000 or so perished in total. Krakatoa itself then slumped into the boiling depths of the ocean, but a new island at the site was spotted in 1927, and it still occasionally spits lava into the sky. It has been dubbed Anak Krakatoa, or Child of Krakatoa.

Mount St. Helens

Mount St. Helens was getting ready to burst for nearly two months before it exploded, not to mention the more than 120 years it lay dormant. While the eruption was anticipated, the manner in which it occurred was completely unprecedented. At 8:32 a.m. on May 18, 1980, a 5.1-magnitude earthquake triggered a sideways blast that swept the mountain's north face away into a cascading landslide that shot hot ash and stone out some 15 miles at speeds of at least 300 mph. At the same time, a mushroom-shaped plume of ash shot 16 miles into the air, eventually covering three states. Complete darkness blanketed Spokane, Wash, a city about 250 miles northeast of the volcano. When the ash came down it fell in the form of black rain that literally coated the residents of Washington, Idaho and parts of Montana with a fine gray powder. Fifty-seven people and thousands of animals were killed, and some 200 square miles of trees were obliterated. In 1982, Congress and President Ronald Reagan designated the surrounding land as the Mount St. Helens National Volcanic Monument.

Mount Tambora

The Volcanic Explosivity Index goes up to 8. On that scale, the 1815 eruption of Mount Tambora rates a very destructive 7. The explosion took place on the island of Sumbawa (then in the Dutch East Indies, now in Indonesia) and plunged the region into darkness, but its effects were anything but isolated. Tens of thousands of people were killed by the apocalyptic eruption, subsequent tsunamis and ensuing starvation and disease. The largest volcanic eruption in recorded history changed the world's climate so much (even crops in Europe and North America failed) that 1816 became known as "the year without a summer." Tambora itself shrank several thousand feet and traded its peak for a massive crater at its summit.

Mauna Loa

It is fitting that the state created out of a chain of volcanic islands would be home to the world's largest volcano. Mauna Loa is located on the Big Island of Hawaii and in addition to being the largest, with a summit nearly 13,700 feet high, it is also one of the world's most active. Since 1843, Mauna Loa has erupted 33 times, most recently in 1984. At 60 miles long and 30 miles wide, Mauna Loa, the name of which fittingly means "Long Mountain" in Hawaiian, takes up about half of the Big Island. Its mass also amounts to 85% of all the other Hawaiian Islands combined.

Eyjafjallajokull

It was like an overly contrived disaster flick: A mammoth cloud of ash from an Icelandic volcano creeps across the European continent, shutting down airports and stranding hundreds of thousands for days. Eyjafjallajokull, whose name means 'Island Mountain Glacier' in Icelandic, first erupted this year on March 20,

2011. But it was the eruption that began April 14 that wrought all the havoc, ultimately costing the airline industry more than $1 billion. Across the globe, people cursed the volcano — or attempted to, since few can actually pronounce the name Eyjafjallajokull. And despite all our technological prowess, human ingenuity is shown to be futile in the face of an ash plume.

Mount Pelée

Mount Pelée, standing more than 4,500 feet high on the French Caribbean island of Martinique, erupted violently in May 1902, killing nearly 30,000 people — effectively the entire port city of St. Pierre. The catastrophe was so devastating that the term *pelean* — to describe that particular kind of ash, gas and fiery cloud eruption — became part of volcanic vernacular. There had been warnings of steam, light earth shocks and raining ash, but they were ignored. After the town was wiped out, Pelée went dormant for some months, until geologists discovered a lava dome, dubbed the tower of Pelée, that rose to more than 1,000 feet above the crater floor before eventually crumbling in March 1903.

Thera

Some 3,500 years ago, an event of cataclysmic proportions rocked the Mediterranean. The volcano at Thera (later known as the Greek island of Santorini) exploded with what is estimated at four to five times the eruptive force of Krakatoa in 1883, blowing a hole into the Aegean isle and sending out shock waves that, according to historians, would reverberate for centuries to come. The great seafaring Minoan civilization, the dominant Greek culture of the time, potentially withered away after clouds of ash enveloped its cities and great tsunami waves smashed its fleets. Stories of a world-shaking eruption linger in legends across the Mediterranean. For years, adventure-seeking archaeologists have even pored through Thera's geological record in search of the fabled lost city of Atlantis. Ancient Egyptian stela from roughly the same era chronicle a volcanic storm that "caused darkness in the Western region" and "annihilated" towns and temples alike. And some biblical scholars have even suggested Thera's destructive effects underlie the Old Testament's tales of God-sent plagues and devastation.

Nevado del Ruiz

The eruption was small — in volcanic terms, that is — producing only about 3% of the ash ejected by Mount St. Helens in 1980. Instead, it was the mudflows that made Colombia's 1985 Nevado del Ruiz explosion the second deadliest in the 20th century and the fourth deadliest in recorded history. The volcano has been blowing its top since the Pleistocene era and has erupted three times in modern history, including in 1595 and 1845. But on November 13, 1985, a relatively small explosion unleashed floods that swept away 1,500 people on one side of the mountain. On the other side was the town of Armero, the site of the worst destruction. 25-m.p.h. lahars (volcanic mudflows) obliterated the town and blanketed it in gray muck. When the landslides subsided, 23,000 people had died and damage was estimated at $1 billion — one-fifth of Colombia's GNP at the time.

Philippines: Mount Pinatubo volcanic eruption

Mount Pinatubo is an active volcano situated on the isle of Luzon in the Philippine, on the borders of the Pampagna, Balaan and Zambales provinces. After more than 500 years of dormancy, the volcano erupted in 1991, producing the largest and most violent eruption of the 20th century. Volcanic activity in the Pinatubo was triggered by a series of earthquakes in the area. It caused a 7 km-high atmospheric ash column containing 5 billion cubic metres of ash. Ashes reached heights of up to 30 km at the peak of the eruption.

Volcanic deposits, ashes and mudflows destroyed much of the area surrounding the volcano. Thousands of houses were demolished in the eruption. The ash cloud from the volcano covered an area of some 125,000 km , bringing total darkness to much of central Luzon.

The Philippine Institute of Volcanology and Seismology led by Raymundo Punongbayan issued a warning indicating the possibility of a major eruption within two weeks. As a result of the institute's predictions of the volcanic eruption and the warning, approximately 200,000 people could be evacuated on time. If these predictions had not been made, the volcanic eruption would have led to tens of thousands of deaths. The number of deaths was limited to 847. Another 173 people were injured and 23 went missing. Roofs collapsing under the weight of accumulated wet ash killed most people. Starvation was also a noted cause of death because arable land was covered in ash and there was no harvest. Livestock was killed massively during the eruptions. Damage to health facilities in the area caused people to die from disease because of overdue hospitalization.

The eruption emitted thousands of tonnes of aerosols into the atmosphere, causing the impact to be noticeable all over the world. Some 15 million tons of sulphur dioxides were emitted, resulting in acid rain from sulphuric acid formation and in cooling of the earth's temperature by 1 deg. C. It also increased ozone layer destruction.

The eruption of Mount Pinatubo severely hampered the economic development of the surrounding areas. It cost billions of dollars to repair the damage to surrounding cities. Education and working facilities were disrupted. In all, the eruption ejected about ten cubic kilometres (2.5 mile) of material, making it the largest eruption since that of Novarupta in 1912 and some ten times larger than the 1980 eruption of Mount St. Helens.

Other volcanic eruptions

Volcanic eruptions have been recorded long before the 20th century, for example Vesuvius in Italy in 79 AD. This eruption ruined the cities of Pompeii and Herculaneum and killed 15,000 people. Even now, volcanic eruptions still occur.

Some of the eruptions recorded in the past centuries are listed below:

1586 Kelut, Indonesia – caused 10,000 deaths

1631 Vesuvius, Italy – caused 3,500 deaths

1772 Papandayan, Indonesia – caused 3,000 deaths

1783 Asama, Japan – caused 1.377 deaths

1783 Laki, Iceland – 9,350 deaths, most due to starvation

1792 Mount Unzen, Japan – caused tsunami and 14,300 deaths

1815 Tambora, Indonesia – 92,000 deaths, caused by starvation and disease

1882 Galunggung, Indonesia – caused 4,000 deaths

1883 Krakatau, Indonesia – caused tsunami and 36,417 deaths

1902 Mount Pelée, West Indies – devastation of St. Pierre and 40,000 deaths

1919 Kelut, Indonesia – caused 5,110 deaths

1951 Lamington, Papua New Guinea – caused 3,000 deaths

1963 Aguna, Indonesia – caused 1,184 deaths

1982 El Chichon, Mexico – caused 2,000 deaths

1985 Nevado del Ruiz, Columbia – deadly mudflow, 25,000 deaths

1991 Mount Unzen, Japan

1994 Rabaul, Papua New Guinea

1997 Soufrière Hills, Montserrat, West Indies

2004 Manam, Indonesia – 10,000 people evacuated, most still living in temporary camps

Chapter – 8

Nuclear Radiations

The nuclear debate is growing in importance as governments everywhere are looking for ways to maintain economic growth and reduce the effects of global warming. But it now looks like the disadvantages are just too great. Nuclear radiation, by definition, are not only the evil rays that escape from nuclear energy reactors or nuclear bombs. Nuclear radiation is everywhere and some of it is beneficent. The sun's energy comes from nuclear fusion. Geothermal energy comes from the heat of radioactive rock deep down in the earth. And cosmic radiation constantly "bombards" the earth. Natural nuclear energy reactors have even been documented in Africa.

Radiation is actually nothing more than the emission of energy waves through space as well as through physical objects. In other words, radiation is energy in the process of being transmitted, which may take such forms as light, or tiny particles much too small to see. Visible light, the ultra-violet light we receive from the sun and from sun-beds, and transmission signals for TV and radio communications are all forms of radiation that are common in our daily lives. These are all referred to as 'non-ionizing' radiation.

Radiation particularly associated with nuclear medicine and the use of nuclear energy, along with X-rays, is 'ionizing' radiation, which means that the radiation has sufficient energy to interact with matter, especially the human body, and produce ions, *i.e.* it can eject an electron from an atom. Usually 'ionizing' and 'non-ionizing' radiation are electromagnetic radiation and these are classified into the following types:

- Radio waves
- Infrared waves
- Visible light
- Ultraviolet waves
- X-ray
- Gamma rays and
- Cosmic rays

X-rays from a high-voltage discharge were discovered in 1895. Radioactivity from the decay of elements was discovered by French scientist Henri Becquerel in 1896. Becquerel found that his photographic plates had become fogged, even though they had been protected from light. What this meant was that another source with properties of light had penetrated the plates' covering. He concluded that this effect came from compounds that he was working with and which contained uranium. Materials with such properties are called *radioactive* and include uranium, thorium and potassium. The actual radioactivity is the result of radioactive decay.

Many scientists then undertook study of these, and especially their medical applications. This led to the identification of different kinds of radiation from the decay of atomic nuclei, and understanding of the nature of the atom. Neutrons were identified in 1932, and in 1939 atomic fission was discovered by irradiating uranium with neutrons, and this led on to harnessing the energy released by fission.

There are three types of radiation with varying abilities to penetrate objects or bodies. These are

- Alpha
- Beta, and
- Gamma radiation

You can shield yourself from alpha radiation by something as flimsy as a sheet of paper. Beta rays need six millimetres of aluminium and gamma rays can be stopped only by dense material, like lead.

Cosmic radiation is produced by nuclear fusion occurring in the sun and stars in the universe. Its rays are made up of high-energy electrons, neutrons and nuclei of very short wavelengths. These travel easily through an inch of lead. And the higher you are in the earth's atmosphere the more exposed you are to these rays because the further they travel into our atmosphere the more they are slowed down. Astronauts are exposed to high levels of cosmic radiation. Cosmic radiation can alter DNA in the cells of human and animal bodies.

Radiation can damage cells and the DNA inside them through its ionizing effect. This effect happens when a particle carrying high energy such as photon removes an electron from its orbit within an atom's nucleus, thereby changing the properties of the atom. If enough ionization occurs, it damages the DNA, cell and tissue. A common effect of this type of ionization is sunburn that is caused by the ultraviolet light of the sun. Excessive exposure to ultraviolet light can cause mutations in human cells leading to melanoma and other cancers. Of course, the ionizing effects of the nuclear radiation from radioactive materials can do the same thing. X-rays, gamma rays and far ultraviolet light are always ionizing. Near ultraviolet light and visible light ionize only some molecules. Radio waves and microwaves do not have any ionizing effect.

Beneficial effects of nuclear radiation

Nuclear radiation has a number of beneficial uses, as listed below:

- Medicinal, such as radio therapy for cancers and X-rays
- Dating purposes
- Level indicators and thickness gauges
- In smoke detectors and
- In tracing locations of gas or liquid leaks
- In tracing locations of malfunctioning in the body such as a blocked kidney
- Sterilisation of medical instruments or bacteria or moulds in foods

These and other such applications involve use of low levels of radioactive compounds. However, repeated exposure to X-rays is hazardous to your health because of the ionizing effects of nuclear radiation.

All radioactive substances decay over time. Some take fractions of seconds, others thousands of years. In theory all radioactive substances stay slightly radioactive and are never completely inert. That's why it is more appropriate to use the 'half-life' of a radioactive substance to indicate its level of radioactivity. The half life of a radioactive substance is the time it takes for its radioactivity to fall by half. For example, if the radioactivity of a radioactive substance falls by half every two years, its half life would be two years. It would take much longer for its radioactivity to fall to very low levels and that after six years it would have dropped to one-eighth of its radioactivity. At every step of its decay, a radioactive substance transforms into another substance as the composition of the nuclei in its atoms changes. The half life of uranium 238 is 4.5 billion years. That means that within that time only half of the uranium 238 will decay.

In nuclear bomb explosions or nuclear reactor accidents, radioactive iodine can be dispersed over wide geographic areas. In the case of the Chernobyl nuclear accident radioactive iodine was dispersed as far as 500 km. We do not know the extent of iodine radiation leaked from Japan's Fukushima nuclear power plant following an explosion after the March 2011 earthquake, but its effects may be global. Thyroid cancer is one result of iodine radiation.

There is a means to escape the dangerous effect of iodine radiation but it has to be used before exposure to iodine radiation. Taking potassium iodide (KI) or potassium iodate (KIO_3) will saturate the thyroid gland with the safe and stable iodine, contained in these chemicals. This leaves no room for the radioactive iodine to be taken up in the thyroid. Therefore any ingested or inhaled iodine is rapidly eliminated via the kidneys.

Given that there are some 440 nuclear reactors worldwide, one would expect a high risk of radioactive radiation. However, the only major nuclear accident that saw radiation escape over large areas has to date been Chernobyl. A small number of people died in the Chernobyl accident and there are various estimates of how many people have been affected from the Chernobyl effects in the long term. It should be pointed out that the Chernobyl plant lacked a protective housing unlike almost all other nuclear reactors and that the shut-down procedures followed were contra-indicated.

Distinguished scientist James Lovelock, author of "The Revenge of Gaia: Earth's Climate Crisis," "The Fate of Humanity". and other books, holds that every person on the earth has radioactive elements in their bodies from past nuclear bomb tests. However, he also holds that the cancer rates have not demonstrably risen as a result. According to him, the risks of nuclear energy are minimal and outweigh the risks posed by global warming resulting from the use of fossil fuels.

Of course, others vehemently disagree. Obviously one serious accident is too many, like the March 2011 Japanese earthquake and its effects on nuclear reactors there show. Similarly, each nuclear bomb and a depleted uranium-tipped missile is one too many. Nuclear energy then, like any other energy, has advantages and disadvantages. But perhaps we are now forcibly learning that the disadvantages are too great a risk. The following facts will add to your understanding about nuclear radiation:

- Natural sources account for most of the radiation we all receive each year.
- The nuclear fuel cycle does not give rise to significant radiation exposure for members of the public.
- Radiation protection standards assume that any dose of radiation, no matter how small, involves a possible risk to human health. This deliberate conservative assumption is increasingly being questioned.

Nuclear radiation arises from hundreds of different kinds of unstable atoms. While many exist in nature, the majority are created in nuclear reactions. Ionizing radiation which can damage living tissue is emitted when the unstable atoms (radionuclides) change ('decay') spontaneously to become different kinds of atoms.

Alpha particles

These are helium nuclei consisting of two protons and two neutrons and are emitted from naturally-occurring heavy elements such as uranium and radium, as well as from some man-made transuranic elements. Alpha particles are intensely ionizing but cannot penetrate the skin, so are dangerous only if emitted inside the body.

Beta particles

These are fast-moving electrons emitted by many radioactive elements. Beta particles are more penetrating than alpha particles, but can be easily shielded – they can be stopped by a few millimetres of wood or aluminium. They can penetrate a little way into human flesh but are generally less dangerous to people than gamma radiation. Exposure to beta particles produces an effect like sunburn, but which is slower to heal. Beta-radioactive substances are also safe if kept in appropriate sealed containers.

Gamma rays

These are high-energy beams much the same as X-rays. They are emitted in many radioactive decays and are very penetrating, hence require more substantial shielding. Gamma rays are the main hazard to people dealing with sealed radioactive materials that is used, for example, in industrial gauges and radiotherapy machines. Radiation dose badges are worn by workers in exposed situations to detect them and hence monitor exposure. All of us receive about 0.5-1 mSv per year of gamma radiation from cosmic rays and from rocks, and in some places, much more. Gamma activity in a substance (*e.g.* rock) can be measured with a scintillometer or Geiger counter.

X-rays are also ionizing radiation, virtually identical to gamma rays, but not nuclear in origin. Cosmic radiation consists of very energetic particles, mostly protons, which bombard the earth from outer space. Neutrons are mostly released by nuclear fission (the splitting of atoms in a nuclear reactor), and hence are seldom encountered outside the core of a nuclear reactor. Thus they are not normally a problem outside nuclear plants. Fast neutrons can be very destructive to human tissue.

To quantify how much radiation we are exposed to in our daily lives and assess its potential health impact, it is necessary to establish a unit of measurement. The basic unit of radiation dose absorbed in tissue is the gray (Gy), where one gray represents the deposition of one joule of energy per kilogram of tissue.

However, since neutrons and alpha particles cause more damage per gray than gamma or beta radiation, another unit, the sievert (Sv), is used in setting radiological protection standards. This unit of measurement takes into account biological effects of different types of radiation. One gray of beta or gamma radiation has one sievert of biological effect, one gray of alpha particles has 20 Sv effect and one gray of neutrons is equivalent to around 10 Sv (depending on their energy). Since the sievert is a relatively large value, dose to humans is normally measured in millisieverts (mSv), one-thousandth of a sievert.

The becquerel (Bq) is a unit or measure of actual radioactivity in material (as distinct from the radiation it emits, or the human dose from that), with reference to the number of nuclear disintegrations per second (1 Bq = 1 disintegration/sec). Quantities of radioactive material are commonly estimated by measuring the amount of intrinsic radioactivity in becquerels. One Bq of radioactive material is that amount which has an average of one disintegration per second, *i.e.* an activity of 1 Bq.

Radiation can arise from human activities or from natural sources. Most radiation exposure is from natural sources. These include radioactivity in rocks and soil of the earth's crust; radon, a radioactive gas given out by many volcanic rocks and uranium ore; and cosmic radiation. The human environment has always been radioactive and accounts for up to 85% of the annual human radiation dose.

Radiation arising from human activities typically accounts for up to 15% of the public's exposure every year. This radiation is no different from natural radiation except that it can be controlled. X-rays and other medical procedures account for most exposure from this quarter. Less than 1% of exposure is due to the fallout from past testing of nuclear weapons or the generation of electricity in nuclear as well as coal and geothermal power plants.

Backscatter X-ray scanners being introduced for airport security will give exposure of up to 5 microsieverts (ìSv), compared with 5 ìSv on a short flight and 30 ìSv on a long intercontinental flight across the equator, or more at higher latitudes – by a factor of 2 or 3. Aircrew can receive up to about 5 mSv/yr from their hours in the air, while frequent flyers can score a similar increment. In the UK, the National Radiation Protection Board's 1999 survey showed that on average, nuclear power workers received a lower annual radiation dose than flight crew, and frequent flyers in 250 hours would receive 1 mSv.

The maximum annual dose allowed for radiation workers is 20 mSv/yr, though in practice doses are usually kept well below this level. In comparison, the average dose received by the public from nuclear power is 0.0002 mSv/yr, which is of the order of 10,000 times smaller than the total yearly dose received by the public from background radiation.

Naturally occurring background radiation is the main source of exposure for most people, and provides some perspective on radiation exposure from nuclear energy. The average dose received by all of us from background radiation is around 2.4 mSv/yr, which can vary depending on the geology and altitude where people live – ranging between 1 and 10 mSv/yr, but can be more than 50 mSv/yr. The highest known level of background radiation affecting a substantial population is in Kerala and Madras states in India where some 140,000 people receive doses which average over 15 millisievert per year from gamma radiation, in addition to a similar dose from radon. Comparable levels occur in Brazil and Sudan, with average exposures up to about 40 mSv/yr to many people.

Several places are known in Iran, India and Europe where natural background radiation gives an annual dose of more than 50 mSv and up to 260 mSv (at Ramsar in Iran). Lifetime doses from natural radiation range up to several thousand millisievert. However, there is no evidence of increased cancers or other health problems arising from these high natural levels. Radon gas has decay products that are alpha emitters. People everywhere are typically exposed to around 0.2 mSv/yr, and often up to 3 mSv/yr, from inhaled radon without apparent ill-effect. However, in industrial situations its control is a high priority.

Public dose limits for exposure from uranium mining or nuclear plants are usually set at 1 mSv/yr above background.

In most countries the current maximum permissible dose to radiation workers is 20 mSv per year averaged over five years, with a maximum of 50 mSv in any one year. This is over and above background exposure, and excludes medical exposure. The value originates from the International Commission on Radiological Protection (ICRP), and is coupled with the requirement to keep exposure as low as reasonably achievable (ALARA) – taking into account social and economic factors.

Radiation protection at uranium mining operations and in the rest of the nuclear fuel cycle is tightly regulated, and levels of exposure are monitored.

There are four ways in which people are protected from identified radiation sources:

- **Limiting time:** In occupational situations, dose is reduced by limiting exposure time.
- **Distance:** The intensity of radiation decreases with distance from its source.
- **Shielding**: Barriers of lead, concrete or water give good protection from high levels of penetrating radiation such as gamma rays. Intensely radioactive materials are therefore often stored or handled under water, or by remote control in rooms constructed of thick concrete or lined with lead.
- **Containment**: Highly radioactive materials are confined and kept out of the workplace and environment. Nuclear reactors operate within closed systems with multiple barriers which keep the radioactive materials contained.

Radiation protection standards are based on the conservative assumption that the risk is directly proportional to the dose, even at the lowest levels, though there is no actual evidence of harm at low levels. This assumption, called the 'linear no-threshold (LNT) hypothesis', is recommended for radiation protection purposes only, such as setting allowable levels of radiation exposure of individuals. It cannot properly be used for predicting the consequences of an actual exposure to low levels of radiation. For example, it suggests that if the dose is halved from a high level where effects have been observed, there will be half the effect, and so on. This would be very misleading if applied to a large group of people exposed to trivial levels of radiation and could lead to inappropriate actions to avert the doses.

Much of the evidence which has led to today's standards derives from the atomic bomb survivors in 1945, who were exposed to high doses incurred in a very short time. In setting occupational risk estimates, some allowance has been made for the body's ability to repair damage from small exposures, but for low-level radiation exposure the degree of protection may be unduly conservative.

In any country, radiation protection standards are set by government authorities, generally in line with recommendations by the International Commission on Radiological Protection (ICRP), and coupled with the requirement to keep exposure as low as reasonably achievable (ALARA), taking into account social and economic factors. The authority of the ICRP comes from the scientific standing of its members and the merit of its recommendations.

The three key points of the ICRP's recommendations are:

- **Justification:** No practice should be adopted unless its introduction produces a positive net benefit.
- **Optimisation**: All exposures should be kept as low as reasonably achievable, economic and social factors being taken into account.
- **Limitation**: The exposure of individuals should not exceed the limits recommended for the appropriate circumstances.

National radiation protection standards are framed for both occupational and public exposure categories. The ICRP recommends that the maximum permissible dose for occupational exposure should be 20 millisievert per year averaged over five years (i.e. 100 millisievert in 5 years) with a maximum of 50 millisievert in any one year. For public exposure, 1 millisievert per year averaged over five years is the limit. In both categories, the figures are over and above background levels, and exclude medical exposure.

The average annual radiation dose to employees in uranium mines (in addition to natural background) is around 2 mSv (ranging up to 10 mSv). Natural background radiation is about 2 mSv. In most mines, keeping doses to such low levels is achieved with straightforward ventilation techniques coupled with rigorously enforced procedures for hygiene. In some Canadian mines, with very high-grade ore, sophisticated means are employed to limit exposure. Occupational doses in the US nuclear energy industry – conversion, enrichment, fuel fabrication and reactor operation – average less than 3 mSv/yr.

The March 1979 accident at Three Mile Island in the USA caused some people near the plant to receive very minor doses of radiation, well under the internationally recommended level. Subsequent scientific studies found no evidence of any harm resulting from that exposure. In 1996, some 2,100 lawsuits claiming adverse health effects from the accident were dismissed for lack of evidence.

Immediately after the Chernobyl disaster in 1986, much larger doses were experienced. Apart from the residents of nearby Pripyat, who were evacuated within two days, some 24,000 people living within 15 km of the plant received an average of 450 mSv before they were evacuated.

In June 1989, a group of experts from the World Health Organization agreed that an incremental long-term dose of 350 mSv should be the criterion for relocating people affected by the 1986 Chernobyl accident. This was considered a "conservative value which ensured that the risk to health from this exposure was very small compared with other risks over a lifetime". (For comparison, background radiation averages about 100-200 mSv over a lifetime in most places.)

Regarding the emergency workers with doses lower than those causing ARS symptoms, a 2006 World Health Organization report referred to studies carried out on 61,000 emergency Russian workers where a total of 4995 deaths from this group were recorded during 1991-1998.

"The number of deaths in Russian emergency workers attributable to radiation caused by solid neoplasms and circulatory system diseases can be estimated to be about 116 and 100 cases respectively." Furthermore, although no increase in leukaemia is discernible yet, "the number of leukaemia cases attributable to radiation in this cohort can be estimated to be about 30." Thus, 4.6% of the number of deaths in this group are attributable to radiation-induced diseases. (The estimated average external dose for this group was 107 mSv.)

There has been no increase attributable to Chernobyl in congenital abnormalities, adverse pregnancy outcomes or any other radiation-induced disease in the general population either in the contaminated areas or further afield.

After the shelter was built over the destroyed reactor at Chernobyl, a team of about 15 engineers and scientists was set up to investigate the situation inside it. Over several years they repeatedly entered the ruin, accumulating individual doses of up to 15,000 mSv. Daily dose was mostly restricted to 50 mSv, though occasionally it was many times this. None of the men developed any symptoms of radiation sickness, but they must be considered to have a considerably increased cancer risk.

Our knowledge of radiation effects derives primarily from groups of people who have received high doses. The risk associated with large radiation doses is relatively well established. However, the risks associated with doses under about 200 mSv are less obvious because of the large underlying incidence of cancer caused by other factors. Radiation protection standards assume that any dose of radiation, no matter how small, involves a possible risk to human health. However, available scientific evidence does not indicate any cancer risk or immediate effects at doses below 100 mSv a year. At low levels of exposure, the body's natural repair mechanisms seem to be adequate to repair radiation damage to cells soon after it occurs.

Epidemiological studies continue on the survivors of the atomic bombing of Hiroshima and Nagasaki, involving some 76,000 people exposed at levels ranging up to more than 5,000 mSv. These have shown that radiation is the likely cause of several hundred deaths from cancer in addition to the normal incidence found in any population. From this data the International Commission on Radiological Protection (ICRP) and others estimate the fatal cancer risk as 5% per sievert exposure for a population of all ages – so one person in 20 exposed to 1,000 mSv could be expected to develop a fatal cancer some years later. In Western countries, about a quarter of people die from cancers, with smoking, dietary factors, genetic factors and strong sunlight being among the main causes. Radiation is a weak carcinogen, but undue exposure can certainly increase health risks.

In 1990, the US National Cancer Institute (NCI) found no evidence of any increase in cancer mortality among people living near to 62 major nuclear facilities. The NCI study was the broadest of its kind ever conducted and supported similar studies conducted elsewhere in the USA as well as in Canada and Europe.

In the UK there are significantly elevated childhood leukaemia levels near Sellafield as well as elsewhere in the country. The reasons for these increases, or clusters, are unclear, but a major study of those near Sellafield has ruled out any contribution from nuclear sources. Apart from anything else, the levels of radiation at these sites are too low to account for the excess incidences reported. However, studies are continuing in order to provide more conclusive answers.

Some evidence suggests that there may be a threshold below which no harmful effects of radiation occur. However, this is not yet accepted by national or international radiation protection bodies as sufficiently well-proven to be taken into official standards.

A November 2009 technical report from the Electric Power Research Institute in the USA drew upon more than 200 peer-reviewed publications on effects of low-level radiation and concluded that the effects of low dose-rate radiation are different and that "the risks due to [those effects] may be over-estimated" by the linear hypothesis. "From an epidemiological perspective, individual radiation doses of less than 100 mSv in a single exposure are too small to allow detection of any statistically significant excess cancers in the presence of naturally occurring cancers. The doses received by nuclear power plant workers fall into this category because exposure is accumulated over many years, with an average annual dose about 100 times less than 100 mSv". It quoted the US Nuclear Regulatory Commission that "since 1983, the US nuclear industry has monitored more than 100,000 radiation workers each year, and no workers have been exposed to more than 50 mSv in a year since 1989."

In addition, there is increasing evidence of beneficial effect from low-level radiation (up to about 10 mSv/yr). This 'radiation hormesis' may be due to an adaptive response by the body's cells, the same as that with other toxins at low doses. In the case of carcinogens such as ionizing radiation, the beneficial effect is seen both in lower incidence of cancer and in resistance to the effects of higher doses. However, until possible mechanisms are confirmed, uncertainty will remain. Further research is under way and the debate continues. Meanwhile, standards for radiation exposure continue to be deliberately conservative.

Chernobyl Nuclear Disaster

On April 26, 1986 tests were conducted in nuclear reactor 4 of the Chernobyl nuclear power plant in Ukraine, located 80 miles from Kiev. These tests required part of the security system to be shut down. Errors in the reactor design and errors in judgment of the personnel of the power plant caused cooling water to start boiling. This caused reactor stress, resulting in energy production increases to ten times the normal level. Temperatures reached more than 2000 °C, causing fuel rod melting and further boiling of cooling water.

Extreme pressures in cooling water pipes resulted in cracks, which caused steam to escape. At 1:23h in the middle of the night the escaped steam caused an explosion slamming off the roof of the building, starting a major fire and simultaneously forming an atmospheric cloud containing approximately 185 to 250 million curies of radioactive material.

Fire and explosion instantly killed 31 people. Two days after the explosion, the Swedish national radio reported that 10.000 times the normal amount of cesium-137 existed in the atmosphere, prompting Moscow to officially respond. The following day over 135,000 people were evacuated from within a 30 km radius of the accident site. This area was labelled the 'special zone'. The evacuation from the special zone was permanent, as the high levels of radioactivity have been predicted to exist there for several centuries.

The radioactive cloud was blown north and northwest by wind, causing the first mention of the accident after radioactivity measurements in Sweden. The cloud covered a large area in Europe. On May 2, the cloud even reached the Netherlands, causing fresh fruit and vegetable consumption to be prohibited.

There are many estimates concerning the number of victims that suffer from symptoms induced by radiation. Reliable data is still lacking. The World Health Organization (WHO) stated that approximately 800,000 people have worked on fire extinguishing, restoring the reactor and cleaning up pollution in the first year after the accident. These people only remained in the area for short periods of time to prevent health problems. Ukrainian government figures show that more than 8.000 Ukrainians have died as a result of exposure to radiation during the first cleanup operation. It is stated that the eventual death toll resulting from the nuclear explosion ranges from 30 to 300,000 and many unofficial sources put the toll over 400,000.

The people that have lived in the Chernobyl area during the accident suffer from various health problems. Immediately after the accident, hundreds of people were diagnosed with radiation sickness. Particularly in Belarus, there has been a dramatic increase in the number of thyroid cancers (2400%) and leukaemia (100%).

Children of Chernobyl victims suffer from birth defects (250% increase), causing cancer and heart diseases. Approximately 64% of all Ukrainian children under 15 suffering from cancer lived in the most contaminated areas. Genetic defects often result in mutations causing missing limbs.

The extraordinary increase in the number of these illnesses can be associated with the exposure of the population to the aggressive radioactive particles released by the Chernobyl explosion. Among these were the following four dangerous substances, which are not identified as such by our bodies:

- **Plutonium** is recognized as iron by the human body and distributed by the blood system. It causes cancer and blood disorders. It has a half-life of 24,400 years and will be present in a 30 km radius around the Chernobyl site for many centuries to come.
- **Cesium 137** is mistaken for potassium and is absorbed by the muscles.
- **Iodine 131** is not recognized as a radioactive substance and is therefore absorbed by the thyroid

gland. It causes thyroid cancer, particularly in children between 0 and 18 years old. An operation can save the children, but a scar known as the 'Belarussian Necklace' marks them as Chernobyl victims forever.

- **Strontium 90** is recognized by the body as calcium and causes leukaemia upon distribution throughout the bone structure.

After the explosion, reactor 4 was wrapped in a concrete sarcophagus in November 1986 to protect the area. After some time the other three reactors where running again. In 1989 the construction of a 5th and 6th reactors was abandoned. There was some discussion going on about the safety of the sarcophagus of reactor 4. In the long run, this would not be a very solid construction and according to many it must be replaced. We now know that this replacement must be carried out soon, because the reactor has begun to leak radiation. Holes and fissures in the structure now cover 1,000 square metres. These cracks and holes are further exacerbated by the intense heat inside the reactor, which is still over 200 degrees Celsius.

After the Chernobyl disaster, international organizations pressured the Ukrainian government to close the remaining reactors. This was disadvantageous for the country because it derived 5% of its power supply from the power plant. Eventually, it was decided that the power plant would be closed in winter of the year 2000. The Ukrainian government tried to obtain a postponement, but the reactor was nevertheless closed in December 2000.

Dangerous chemicals emitted by the nuclear power plant after the explosion continue to spread by bushfires and weather conditions, re-contaminating soil, air and water. New radiation hot spots are still being discovered in Belarus and Ukraine and evacuations will need to continue well into the 21st century.

Twenty-five years on, Chernobyl nuclear power plant signifies the worst nuclear accident in history. It was a disaster whose aftershocks are, in many ways, still felt. More than two million people in Ukraine and 1.8 million in Belarus still grapple with radiation-related health issues as well as mental and social trauma even as question marks remain about the incident.

Considerable confusion remains over the exact events of that fateful day. In order to find answers, Marples visited Chernobyl a few times. Initially, the accident was concealed from the public on Moscow's orders, specifically at the instance of the Ministry of Medium Machine Building, the Soviet ministry responsible for nuclear weapons. "The Chernobyl station was under this ministry, as originally the reactors were linked to weapons production before they were modified to the civilian programme. The ostensible reason for official silence, repeated ad nauseam by Soviet officials, was to prevent panic," he says.

The continuing secrecy means that even the sequence of events of that dreadful night remains unknown. Marples muses that the problem must have started when safety devices were dismantled in order to prevent the reactor shutting down as part of an experiment. He conjectures that "an operator made an error that caused power to drop below the 30 % needed for the experiment. The reactor went down to 1 %, power began to rise because of coolant boiling, and he (the operator) decided to drive in the emergency rods to shut down the reactor, which was by now very unstable. The subsequent power surge resulted in two explosions that blew the top off the reactor, scattering graphite and fuel, and starting more than 30 fires."

Radiation from the fires was so intense that the Wormwood pine forest in the reactor's vicinity immediately turned a red-brown and died, earning it the new name of

'Red Forest'. Today, the area around Chernobyl largely consists of deserted villages. Estimates vary but just about 250 mainly elderly people are thought still to live in a place that's believed to be one of the most contaminated in the, world.

Chernobyl cleanup will remain expensive and anxiety-provoking for decades to come. The Ukrainian government organized four days of conferences to mark the 25th anniversary of the April 26, 1986, blast that sent radioactive fallout over much of Europe. An international donors' conference raised pledges of 550 million euros to build a shelter to cover the exploded reactor building for the next century. But that was short of the 740 million euros sought for the shelter and a facility for storing spent reactor fuel. Once the enormous shelter is completed and slid over the reactor building on rails, expected in 2015, workers can begin disassembling the reactor and disposing the hundreds of tons of radioactive material inside. It is still not clear how that will be done or how much it will cost.

Chapter – 9

Mines Explosions

Mining is a dangerous industry and has resulted in thousands of deaths caused by a variety of hazards including coal dust explosions, methane gas, rock falls and carbon monoxide poisoning as well as long-term health problems such as black lung.

Described below are the top ten mining disasters as determined by the number of fatalities. However it needs to be remembered that accurate death tolls were not always available because sometimes bodies could not be recovered, or actual figures of fatalities were not revealed because of political reasons.

Honkeiko Colliery, China (26 April, 1942)

China has arguably the worst mining record in the world with statistics showing that miners are 350 more times likely to die there than anywhere else. There are still mining deaths occurring in China, but the worst occurred in Honkeiko (or Benxihu) Colliery in 1942. When the entrance to the mine collapsed because of a coal dust explosion, thousands of workers were trapped, and 1,549 were estimated to have died. In an effort to contain the blaze, the authorities switched off ventilation, and sealed the mine's entrance, suffocating the trapped workers.

Courrieres, France (10 March, 1906)

An estimated 1,099 miners died (including many children) in what was the worst ever pit disaster in Europe. A large dust explosion devastated the mine shortly after 6:30am on Saturday, 10 March, 1906.

Kyushu, Japan (15 December, 1914)

A deadly gas explosion at the Mitsubishi Hojyo coal mine in Kyushu, Japan, killed 687 miners, making it the worst mining disaster in Japan's history.

Senghenydd, Wales (14 October, 1913)

During a time of record coal production, Welsh mining was dogged by poor safety standards with several deadly accidents happening in the early part of the 20th century. The worst was at Senghenydd, Wales where 438 men and boys were killed by a methane explosion ignited by coal dust. Only 72 bodies were recovered.

Coalbrook, South Africa (1 January, 1960)

This tragedy is the deadliest mining accident in South Africa's history. But the fatalities could have been prevented had the authorities not been negligent in their duty. A rock fall trapped miners in a section of the mine, but since the mining company was not equipped with a drill large enough to create an exit for them, there was no way to escape. 437 miners perished. To add to this blunder, there had been reports that supervisors sent miners exiting the tunnel after earlier rock falls back into the mine.

Wankie, Rhodesia (6 June, 1972)

An methane explosion occurred in an extraction panel underneath a mountain called Madumabisa (Wankie No. 2 Colliery) at 10:30 am on 6, June 1972. The initial explosion was followed shortly after by a coal dust explosion that swept through the mine at such an incredible speed that not one of the 426 miners stood a chance to survive.

Dhanbad, India (28 May, 1965)

A disaster occurred on May 28, 1965 at Dhori colliery in Bermo near Dhanbad in the Jharkand (then Bihar) state of India. On the fateful day, an explosion in Dhori colliery led to a fire in the mines. The fire killed 375 miners.

Barnsley, England (12 December, 1866)

Several explosions ripped through the Oaks mine at Barnsley killing all but six of the 340 miners working at the time. Several other employees of the colliery and rescuers were killed in the blasts that followed bringing the total number of deaths to 361. A furnace man had a remarkable escape having being knocked to the ground by the force of the explosion. He was discovered by rescuers, unconscious, but with a dead cat in his arms.

Monongah, West Virginia, USA (6 December, 1907)

Believed to be the reason for Father's Day, the Monongah mining disaster is the worst in American history killing 361 miners. An explosion ripped through the network of mines with such speed and force that some bodies were discovered with food still in their mouths. The official death toll is said to be very conservative with some estimating the total was more than 600, with horrific stories of workers as young as 13 being caught up in the resulting blaze.

Chasnala, India (27 December, 1975)

A coal mine in Chasnala near Dhanbad experienced a deadly explosion on 27 December, 1975 in the Jharkhand (then Bihar) state of India. The explosion resulted in the caving in of a roof of coal that let in 7,000,000 gallons of water per minute, flooding the mine that was 450-500 metres underground. Miners were trapped under a mountain of debris and drowned when the water surged into the mine. The official death toll was 372. The miners' fate was sealed by the fact that the oxygen level inside the mine was very low while the levels of carbon dioxide and methane gas were very high.

Poor Mining and Coal Mines Nationalisation in India

The Chasnala tragedy once again highlighted the poor conditions in mines.

Nothing seems to have changed as far conditions in mines are concerned. The globalisation and sophisticated technology could not change the fate of the trapped miners and the rest surviving elsewhere in other mines.In all major accidents, the administrative efficiency and technical blunders were exposed badly. At the time of Chasnala disaster, the Dhanbad DGMS claimed to ensure safety measures in all coal mines. But it proved to be a false promise. The investigation on the part of the government always proves to be a cover-up game. The Mining Act, 1955 and the nationalisation of coal mines by the then Prime Minister Indira Gandhi did not help improve the conditions in coal mines. Mine survey reports were not accurate always. Sometimes the survey was accurate, but the mining method faulty, as it happened in Chasnala. Officers responsible for mining and management did care little to go inside the mines. Technically non-professional and almost illiterate mining Sardar (head) was found leading in the operations.

Coal exploration in India even today is largely being carried out by conventional methods of systematic geological mapping followed by drilling, core drilling playing a dominant role. However, in the recent times modern exploration techniques like photo-geology, remote sensing, non-coring drilling and geophysical surveys are being increasingly used for detailed and precise exploration.

From as early as the 1920s, various consultants, commissions and committees had been set up to decide on the question of conservation and scientific exploitation of coal, working conditions in the mines and safety of the work persons, thereby regulate and control the coal industry in India. All of them emphasised the necessity to have state ownership of the coal mines. The overall problem of coking coal in India has been studied in depth by a whole herd of prestigious committees including the Indian Coal Mining Committee (1937), the Indian Coalfields Committee (1946), the Committee on Metallurgical coal conservation (1950).

The architect of coal nationalisation, the late S. Mohan Kumaramangalam, the then Minister of Steel and Mines, had given a vivid description of the mines of Jharia coalfield in his book *Coal Industry in India*.

"Slaughter mining, lack of conservation and unscientific methods remained characteristic of large areas of the industry. Lack of safety and welfare measures, robbing of pillar of coal, selective, seasonal and shallow depth mining in a haphazard manner, etc. seemed to be the guiding principles of a large number of the private collieries."

Acting on the reports of various committees, the then Prime Minister Indira Gandhi nationalised coal mines in May, 1972. These mines are now operated by M/s. Bharat Coking Coal Limited (BCCL). By Coal Mines (Taking over of Management) Ordinance 1973 the non-coking coal mines were also taken over. These mines were nationalised on May 1, 1973 and brought under the management of the Coal Mines Authority Limited (CMAL). Later on the CMAL and the BCCL were merged and the holding company Coal India Limited (CIL) was formed in November, 1975.

Preventing Mine Disasters from Fire and Effective Emergency Response

The Ninth Conference on Safety in Mines at New Delhi held on 2–3, February 2000 formulated the following recommendations for preventing mine disasters from fire and for effective emergency response in case of mine accidents.

1. Considering the risk of fire, all coal mine companies shall rank their coal mines on a uniform scale according to its risk from fire on scientific basis. Guidelines may be framed by DGMs and circulated to all mining companies.
2. Recognizing the urgent need for making the emergency plan responsive, speedy and effective, each mine shall review the existing emergency plan, at a higher level keeping in view the risk from fire.
3. A tripartite committee may be formed to study the feasibility of establishing rescue rooms in coal mines having high risk of fire and employing more than 350 persons ordinarily employed in a shift below ground may be considered.
4. A tripartite committee may be formed to study the feasibility of storing oxygen type self rescuer at strategic places below ground in coal mines with risk of fire in such scale so as to cater to the needs of persons who can be affected in an emergency may be explored.
5. Each mining company shall formulate and implement structured training programme for development of

awareness and increasing effectiveness of emergency response in case of fire amongst work persons, officials and management.

6. Through sustained and meaningful R&D activities, mining companies and research institutions shall help in creating a better understanding of the complex geo-mining situations leading to the occurrence of fire, which in turn will help in formulating guidelines to combat the problem of fire in an effective manner. Early detection of heating effect of reversal of fan and control of fire, other associated aspects may be studied.

12 Miners Killed in Methane Explosion in a Polish Mine

Twelve miners were killed and fifteen seriously injured on September 18, 2009 in a methane explosion at the Wujek-Slask coal mine in southern Poland. A total of 30 miners were hospitalized after the blast which ripped through the mine in Ruda Slaska-Kochlowice. According to mine authorities, around 40 miners were underground in the area when the blast occurred 1,050 meters below the surface. Twenty-nine escaped to the surface while the remainder were evacuated by mine rescue workers. Several miners sustained serious burns.

The Wujek-Slask coal mine explosion was the worst in Polish mines since the death of 23 miners in November 2006 in a methane blast at the Halemba mine in the same southern Polish community of Ruda Slaska. Several mine managers were on trial in connection with the disaster. Poland's most recent mine accident involved the death of six miners in a methane explosion at the Borynia mine in southern Poland in June 2008.

Disaster Management of a Coal Mine

History of coal mine accidents is rather old in Jharia coalfields, which is largely under the control of Bharat Cooking Coal Ltd.

Of the 50 major accidents that have taken place in coal mines in the past 100 years, 20 occurred in the mines of Jharia coalfields. After nationalisation, 11 major coal mine accidents have taken place. Of these, eight were in Jharia coalfields region.

Safety, however, needs to be a major concern for the companies engaged in coal mining. More so, because over 80 per cent of coal mining is carried out by public sector undertakings which are supposed to be the model employers. This, however, does not seem to be the case. Rather, safety is treated as an avoidable liability. Not only have there been accidents at a nagging frequency, most of the time they have been found to occur due to managerial acts of omission and commission. The accident at the Bagdigi mine of Bharat Coking Coal Limited, Dhanbad, followed by another at Chaitudih mine in Ferbruary 2001 were examples of the authorities' negligence. The accident at the Bagdiggi coal mine on the afternoon of February 2, 2001 resulted in 29 deaths including that of two officers. A week later, another accident occurred in the Chaitudih coal mine resulted in one death with some 100 odd mine workers escaping miraculously.

Mine Safety: An Overview

Organised coal mining began in India in the early 19th century in the Raniganj coalfields of Bengal and spread to other parts of the country in the subsequent decades. Accidents have been taking place ever since. In 1899, the first recorded major accident occurred in the Khost coal mine (now in Pakistan) killing 47 persons. This hastened the process of formulation of safety laws by the then British Government. Consequently, the Mines Act was enacted in 1901. Legislative measures have continued to be enacted since then. Yet, the deathrate in coal mine accidents remains high in comparison to other industries.

Disasters causing 10 or more deaths account 10 per cent of total casualties in coal mine accidents. Coal mine managements may like to state the death rate per 1,000 persons employed has gone down from 050 in 1973 (year of nationalisation) to 0.32 at present. But the fact remains that disasters keep on striking the coal mines at regular intervals. Statistically speaking, the rate works out to be once in every 27 months. While the common refrain of coal mine managements is to dismiss these as acts of god, courts of inquiry probing mine disasters attribute these to human failure. The point, however, is not what caused the disaster. It is how to check them. Or reduce the impact of disasters. With the demand-supply gap in coal likely to be huge, there will be an urgent need for increasing the production but with safety. It will not be easy given the attitude of coal mine bosses.

Causes of Mine Accidents

Classical research suggests that faulty attitude proves to be the most important contributory factor in accidents. Post facto analyses often confirm this. More so, in the case of coal mine accidents. It proved so in the case of Chasnala accident (1975), the biggest so far in the history of coal mines. Three hundred seventy five mine workers met their watery grave for some tonnes of coal that the management should have best avoided to extract. Twenty years later, in 1995, the Gazlitand disaster claimed the lives of around 70 miners.

The same set of circumstances, the same round of motions and the same kind of accidents. The fact is in many cases the seasons also have been the same and month too. The February 2001 tragedy in Badigi once again showed why the mistakes are repeated. The precipitating cause was an explosion to facilitate extraction of coal in the seam near an abandoned waterlogged mine. The impact of the explosion led to the collapse of the barrier between the two. The resultant inrush of huge quantity of water trapped the miners culminating in the tragedy. But the basic cause was disregard of safety considerations for some tonnes of coal. Maybe, to get a pat on their backs from top bosses, the superior officers risk the lives of lesser mortals.

The managerial attitude, then, is the main reason why superiors force misadventure on their subordinates. In the process, the mines visit the accidents. The reports of various courts of inquiry constituted to look into the causes of accidents have almost always held negligence and misadventure as a major cause.

Roof falls account for more than one-third fatalities in coal mines. Interestingly, 60 to 80 percent of these arise from non-adherence to coal mine regulations. Human failures, then, must be examined thoroughly in all accidents. And culpability must be fixed to find the real kingpin. There seems to be an intrinsic feeling in coal mine managers that safety is incompatible with production and productivity. Experience, however, proves that this is not so in the long run. Managers get transferred, but the organisation remains and bears the cost.

Avoiding Future Accidents

Accidents are an intriguing reality for coal mine managements, less understood and even more damaging. They happen and they hurt. Coal mine managements must therefore formulate a sound policy for effective accident management.

Such management must be integrated into a well-formulated safety policy of the company, which includes administrative, legal and technical aspects. Needless to say, there has to be special emphasis on training, motivation and participation not just of the employees of the organisation. Even local residents, if trained well, can play a crucial role in helping the company combat accidents. More than technology, it is the human response that is critical. Even the best of technologies cannot substitute for highly motivated human teams. Mining in the final analysis is akin to war situations and the conventional wisdom is that the more you sweat in the peace the less you bleed in wars. You do not know from where the disaster will strike but you must know what has to be done when it strikes. But this calls for a drastic change in the attitudes of the officers. Misadventures, disregarding warning signals, have almost always been the main cause. Warnings have always preceded the accidents. But mine managers have failed to rake a cue from these warning signals leading to heavy loss of life and property. For safer mining, the mine managers have to learn the lessons from their past mistakes and avoid repeating them.

Chapter – 10

Oil Spill

Unfortunately there are places in the world where oil spills are common place and sometimes intentional they are either hidden behind reasons or just ignored because the public have grown accustomed to them. With the greed of a few this will probably continue until there is no more oil to exploit. Maybe if more people in the world know more about this sort of thing then it can change for the better.

Major oil spills of the 20th and 21st century

At the end of the 20th century and the beginning of the 21st century there have been oil spills all over the world, caused either by naval accidents or during major wars. It is impossible to determine which of these oil spills had the most severe consequences for its environment. Consequently, we will sum up a number of oil spills in this environmental disaster top 10. First, we will describe some events that obtained a lot of media attention.

Amoco Cadiz

In 1978 on March 16 the Liberian super tanker Amoco Cadiz stranded on Portsall Rocks off the coast of Brittany, France because of failure of the steering mechanism at 9:15. Although Captain Pasquale Bandari hoisted the international signal for "Not Under Command" almost immediately, he did not request assistance until 11:20, when his engineer determined that the damage was irreparable. The Amoco Cadiz started drifting to shore where touching the bottom ripped open the hull and storage tanks.

The crew of the tanker was rescued by helicopter, but the ship broke in two releasing 230,000 tons of crude oil, which spread through the English Channel. The oil spill polluted approximately 300 kilometres of coastline, destroying fisheries, oysters and seaweed beds. Beaches of 76 Breton communities were polluted by oil.

This was one of the largest environmental disasters known to men in the 1970's. It would be another ten years before the resulting lawsuits were wound up. In 1988 a US federal judge ordered Amoco Oil Corporation to pay 85,2 million dollars in fines, consisting of 45 million dollars for the costs of the spill and an additional 39 million dollars of interest.

Piper Alpha

On July 6, 1988 an explosion occurred on the oil and gas production platform Piper Alpha of Occidental Petroleum Ltd. and Texaco in the North Sea. Piper Alpha was located on the Piper Oilfield, about 190 kilometres from Aberdeen in 144 metres of water. There were about 240 people working on the platform. The explosion and resulting fire killed 167 of them. It is now said that evacuation plans were inadequate and therefore failed preventing any of the deaths. By the time rescue helicopters arrived, flames over 100 metres in height prevented safe approach. Only 62 workers were pulled from the sea alive.

A nearby platform called Tartan continued to pump gas into the upstream pipelines of Piper Alpha after the explosion because they did not have the authority to shut down production, even when the Piper Alpha caught fire. The released gas caused a second explosion and the fire increased, covering the entire platform.

The Cullen Enquiry was set up in November 1988 to establish the cause of the disaster. It was pointed out that the initial explosion was caused by a leakage of natural gas condensate building up beneath the platform, because of maintenance work on a pump and a related safety valve. It resulted in the ignition of secondary oil fires and the melting of upstream gas pipelines. Piper Alpha's operator, Occidental, was found guilty of having inadequate maintenance procedures.

Gulf War

In August 1990 Iraqi forces invaded Kuwait, starting the Gulf War in which an allegiance of 34 nations worldwide was involved. In January, 1991 of the Gulf War, Iraqi forces committed two environmental disasters. The first was a major oil spill 16 kilometres off the shore of Kuwait by dumping oil from several tankers and opening the valves of an offshore terminal. The second was the setting fire to 650 oil wells in Kuwait.

The apparent strategic goal of the action was to prevent a potential landing by US Marines. American air strikes on January 26 destroyed pipelines to prevent further spillage into the Gulf. This however seemed to make little difference. Approximately one million tons of crude oil was already lost to the environment, making this the largest oil spill of human history. In the spring of 1991, as many as 500 oil wells were still burning and the last oil well was not extinguished until a few months later, in November. The oil spills did considerable damage to life in the Persian Gulf (see picture). Several months after the spill, the poisoned waters killed 20.000 seabirds and had caused severe damage to local marine flora and fauna. The fires in the oil wells caused immense amounts of soot and toxic fumes to enter the atmosphere. This had great effects on the health of the local population and biota for several years. The pollution also had a possible impact on local weather patterns.

Tricolor Ship Collision

In the early hours of December 14, 2002 the Norwegian ship Tricolor collided with the Bahama container ship Kariba in the French Channel. The accident was caused by fog and human errors. The Kariba was heavily damaged, but managed to reach the Antwerp harbour. The crew of Tricolor was rescued by emergency teams, which experienced low visibility that made the rescue operation very hard. Fortunately, nobody was hurt. Despite warning signals on the location of the Tricolor the Nicola collided with the wreck on December 16. The Nicola could be safely removed from the scene but the Tricolor was now much more severely damaged. The ship was declared total loss and Berger Smit started to pump 2,200 tons of oil from the wreck.

In January 2003 the oil tanker Vicky collided with the Tricolor, causing some oil from the Vicky to flow into sea and reach French and Belgium shores. Fortunately damages were limited and the Tricolor did not leak any oil. By the end of January even more extreme weather caused Berger Smit to collide with the Tricolor wreck, which started leaking oil. It became apparent that at least 1,000 tons of oil had leaked away into the Channel. The oil reached France and Belgium, causing thousands of dead seabirds to wash ashore. After this third collision a confederation was ordered by the French government to remove the wreck to prevent further environmental damage. Eventually, the ship was broken into nine small pieces, heaved from the water and carried away.

At this moment the sea soil still contains hundreds of cars wreckages that were once transported by the Tricolor. The freight value was approximately 49 million euros. The ship has an additional value of 40 million euros.

Other

There have been many other accidents involving oil spills throughout the years. Many received not nearly as much media attention as the ones mentioned above. Some more examples of oil spills:

- **1967** Liberian tanker Torrey Canyon spills 120,000 ton oil near Cornwall
- **1968** Witwater tanker spills 14,000 barrels of oil near Panama coast
- **1969** tanker Hamilton trader spills 4,000 barrels of oil in Liverpool Bay, England
- **1970** tanker Arrow spills 77,000 barrels of oil near Nova Scotia, Canada
- **1971** tanker Wafra spills 20,000 barrels of oil near Cape Agulhas, Africa
- **1972** tanker Sea Star catches fire after collision in Gulf of Mexico
- **1974** Dutch tanker Metulla spills 53,000 ton crude oil near South-Chilli
- **1976** Liberian tanker Argo Merchant spilled 29,000 square meters of oil near the Massachusetts coast
- **1976** Spanish tanker Urquillo spills more than 100,000 ton oil near Spain
- **1977** tanker Al Rawdatain spills 7,350 barrels of oil near Genoa, Italy

- **1977** tanker Borug spills 213,692 barrels of oil near the coast of Taiwan
- **1978** Brazilian Marina spills 73,600 barrels of oil near Sao Sebastiao, Brazil
- **1979** Betegeuse spills 14,720 barrels of oil near Bantry Bay, Ireland
- **1979** Ixtoc I exploratory well in Mexico blows out and spills 600,000 tons of oil
- **1984** Alvenus tanker grounds southeast of Cameron, Louisiana and spills 65,000 barrels of oil
- **1985** ARCO Anchorage spills 5,690 barrels of oil near the coast of Washington
- **1986** unknown oil spill reaches the coast of Georgia and is later appointed to the Amazon Vulture tanker
- **1989** Aragon tanker spills 175,000 barrels of oil near Madeira, Portugal
- **1990** tanker American Trader grounds near Huntington Beach, California and spills 9458 barrels of oil
- **1990** Cibro Savannah tanker catches fire and spills 481 square meters of oil
- **1990** Jupiter tanker catches fire in Bay City, Mexico and causes oil spill
- **1990** Mega Borg tanker catches fire and spills 19,000 square meters of oil near Galveston, Texas
- **1991** tanker Bahia Paraiso spills 3,774 barrels of oil near Palmer Station, Antarctica
- **1992** Greek tanker Aegean Sea spills 70,000 ton oil near Galicia
- **1993** Bouchard B 155 tanker spills 1,270 square meters of fuel oil after collision with 2 ships
- **1996** Liberian tanker Sea Empress spills 147,000 ton oil near Wales

- **1999** Maltese tanker Erika spills 30,000 ton oil near Brittany
- **2001** tanker Jessica spills 900 ton oil near the Galapagos Isles
- **2002** Bahamese Prestige spills oil near Galicia

These are but a number of that have occurred throughout history. Unfortunately, there are many more.

The Love Canal chemical waste dump

In 1920 Hooker Chemical had turned an area in Niagara Falls into a municipal and chemical disposal site. In 1953 the site was filled and relatively modern methods were applied to cover it. A thick layer of impermeable red clay sealed the dump, preventing chemicals from leaking out of the landfill.

Love Canal seemed like a regular neighbourhood. The only thing that distinguished this neighbourhood from other was the strange odours that often hung in the air and an unusual seepage noticed by inhabitants in their basements and yards. Children in the neighbourhood often fell ill. Love Canal families regularly experienced miscarriages and birth defects.

Lois Gibbs, an activist, noticed the high occurrence of illness and birth defects in the area and started documenting it. In 1978 newspapers revealed the existence of the chemical waste dump in the Love Canal area and Lois Gibbs started petitioning for closing the school. In August 1978, the claim succeeded and the NYS Health Department ordered closing of the school when a child suffered from chemical poisoning.

When Love Canal was researched over 130 pounds of the highly toxic carcinogenic TCDD, a form of dioxin, was discovered. The total of 20,000 tons of waste present in the landfill appeared to contain more than 248 different species of chemicals. The waste mainly consisted of pesticide residues and chemical weapon; research refuse.

The chemicals had entered homes, sewers, yards and creeks and Gibbs decided it was time for more than 900 families to be moved away from the location. Eventually President Carter provided funds to move all the families to a safer area.

The Baia Mare cyanide spill

Workers in gold mines use cyanide (CN) to purify gold from rocks. This is applied for example in Rumania. At 22:00 hours on January 30, 2000 cyanide used in a gold mine in Baia Mare overflowed into the major river the Some and subsequently into the river Tisza. The cause of the spill was a break in the dam that surrounded a settling basin. This resulted in the release of at least 100,000 cubic meters of water with very high cyanide concentrations. The waste water did not only contain cyanide, but also heavy metals such as Copper, Zinc and lead. Copper concentrations exceeded the heavily polluted threshold 40-160 times, the zinc concentration was twice above this standard and the lead concentration 5-9 times greater.

Cyanide is a very aggressive toxin that can kill people. Consequently, when Rumanian authorities were notified of the spill they immediately raised the alarm. This rapid response prevented any human victims. However, the spill did kill all aquatic plant and animal life for dozens of miles downstream. On February 12 it even impacted the major European river Danube, which receives, water from the Tisza. This caused the impact to be noticeable in Hungary and Serbia, as well. Inhabitants of Belgrado witnessed Danube water full of dead fish flowing by. Up to 100 people, most of them children, have been treated in hospital after eating contaminated fish. The Rumanian media entitled this environmental disaster 'the largest since Chernobyl.

"Environmental organizations claim that large companies take advantage of the flexible environmental regulation in poorer countries such as Rumania. It is stated this results in the occurrence of environmental disasters such as that in Baia Mare. The major owner of the Baia Mare gold mine is an Australian called Brett. He commented the media coverage of the Baia Mare disaster, saying reports were utterly exaggerated. He denies the high rate of fish mortality in the area had anything to do with the gold mine. In Serbia the minister of environment has announced he will sue the ones responsible for the spill. He demands an international trial. Fishery has been banned from the Tisza and the population was recommended not to use the water. This has caused many local residents to suffer from drinking water shortages and has caused some losses in the fishing industry.

The European BSE crisis

Bovine Spongiform Encephalopathy (BSE), is a fatal cow disease. The disease is sometimes called 'mad cow disease' because it causes cows to act strangely and collapse on the spot. It is concentrated mainly in the cow's brain, spinal cord and certain organs such as the spleen.

BSE was caused by feeding cows with meat and bone meal, a high-protein substance obtained from butchered sheep and cows. This was applied in Europe because soybeans, the main ingredient of regular cow feed, was hard to obtain.

The accumulation of prions (proteinaceous infectious par ticks) over many generations caused animals to fall ill, increasing the infectious tissue concentration in newly produced meat. In Europe it was first discovered in British cattle in 1986. Contrarily to other European countries, in

Britain it was not required for the animal feed to undergo a steam boiling process for sterilization. This gave the infectious agents a chance to spread. In 1996 the British mistake came to light and European countries banned the import of British cow meat, causing the British meat industry to suffer major losses.

The ban of British meat export appeared to have been implemented too late and consequently BSE started spreading throughout Europe. Many countries started to test its animals. When BSE was suspected on a farm transporting of animals the meat was banned. The animals were killed and their car cases burned. This may have caused air pollution, because cow incineration was carried out in open air without proper filtering on many occasions.

However, in Germany meat and bone meal was still permitted in cow feed until 2000. This caused an aftermath of the epidemic in 2003. BSE was not only harmful to cows; in 1996 it was discovered that a human equivalent of the fatal brain disease existed. The infection is known as Creutsfeldt Jacobs Disease (CJD). Once infectious prions are activated, the disease runs its course within 12 to 18 months and ultimately results in death. Symptoms include depression, coordination problems, memory loss and mood swings, pain in the limbs, bad headaches, cold extremities, pain in the feet, rashes and short-term memory loss.

It is assumed that humans are affected with the BSE-related disease by consuming the organs and tissues from cattle in which the BSE-causing agents are present. Infection can only occur when consumption cows with BSE are 30 months old or older. Estimates state that 400,000 cattle infected with BSE entered the human food chain in the 1980s. The age of these cows prior to slaughter is unknown.

vCJD killed nearly 90 people in the UK by 2003. Deaths from the disease were also reported in France and Italy. In 2004 a total of 158 Europeans acquired or died from vCJD, most of which were Britain's (148). It is now suspected that slaughtering practices and horticultural fertilization practices may also cause the human variant of BSE, but this is still researched.

The BSE epidemic of 1990-2001 was mainly concentrated in the western European Union countries. The incidences of BSE are relatively small in number, but the discovery of the disease had a dramatic effect on European beef consumption, which fell to 27%. In 2001 the European BSE epidemic ceased, having only an aftermath in Germany in 2003. Even after bringing the BSE epidemic under control people are still being diagnosed with its human variant each year, because of its long incubation period. The full extent of the outbreak may still be unknown.

Spanish waste water spill

On April 25, 1998 the dam of the mining residual tank of a pyrite mine in Aznalcollar, Spain suffered a rupture, releasing sludge and contaminated wastewater. The wastewater entered the Guadiamar River, polluting the river with heavy metls such as: cadmium, lead, zinc and copper. It affected an area of 4,634 hectares, contaminating 2,703 hectares with sludge and 1,931 with acidic water. The river pollution caused cultivation lands and forests to be affected. Harvests were no longer fit for consumption, causing financial problems for farmers in the area. Major fish mortality occurred and birds died as a result of consumption of polluted fish. It took one whole month for the river water to recover to its original state.

After the wastewater flow had entered the river a major cleanup operation started, including the installation of walls to prevent further spreading of contaminants and the removal of contaminated sludge. The pH values of the soil were restored by liming and arsenic was removed by adding iron oxyhydroxides, causing a precipitation reaction.

Company technicians stated that the rupture of the residual tank was caused by a deep landslide, which provoked the movement of a certain section of the wall. Authorities also researched the cause of the disaster. Apparently the dam was a weak construction and warnings of possible breakthrough were neglected. The Canadian/Swedish corporation Buliden was held responsible for the wastewater spill. The company was sentenced to financing the cleanup operation and paying compensation to victims.

The Three Mile Island near nuclear disaster

At approximately 4:00 a.m. on March 28, 1979 the main feed water pumps in the non-nuclear cooling system of reactor 2 of the Three Mile Island nuclear power plant near 'Harrisburg, Pennsylvania failed. This caused cooling water to drain away from the reactor resulting in partial melting of the reactor core. Operator errors, a stuck valve, faulty sensors and design errors together resulted in a release of approximately one thousandth as much radiation as during the Chernobyl explosion.

Fortunately about 18 billion curies of radiation that could have been released were held by the containment structure around the reactor This caused some advocates to think that serious nuclear accidents will not occur in the United States. However, many experts have claimed that only luck kept the accident from being worse. The reactor core, according to them, was only just short of becoming hot enough to totally melt down. Complete meltdown was only prevented by immediate implementation of safety measures.

It is very uncertain how much radiation was exactly released at the nuclear accident. It is estimated that this was about 2.5 million curies. A few days after the accident had occurred all children and pregnant women were evacuated from an 8 k.m. radius of three mile Island as a safety precaution.

Radiation from the Three Mile Island reactor has contributed to the premature deaths of some elderly people that lived in the region. Dairy farmers reported that many animals have died consequential to the accident and local residents have developed cancers. Some studies suggested that premature deaths and birth defects also resulted from the nuclear melt-down.

The reactor cleanup started in August 1979 and officially ended in December 1993 at a cost of around 975 million dollars. From 1985 to 1990 almost 100 tonnes of radioactive fuel were removed from the site. Reactor 2 had been online only three months, but now had a ruined reactor vessel and was unsafe to walk in, therefore it has been permanently closed. Reactor 1 was restarted in 1985, but many plans for building new reactors of the same type were dismissed later.

The history of the voyage

Trafigura chartered the Probo Koala under the terms of a time charter entered into on October 25, 2004 between Trafigura Beheer B.V. and Probo Koala Shipping Inc. While the incident at the centre of this inquiry took place in Abidjan, the background has a potentially important impact. As part of their trading operations, Trafigura was carrying out gasoline blending and caustic washing on board the vessel in international waters. This involved the addition of caustic soda and a catalyst to the Probo Koala's naphtha cargo to remove mercaptans. This is a recognised procedure which oil companies adopt to improve naphtha. The slops, which arose as a result of these caustic washing and blending operations, were stored on the Probo Koala in separate tanks.

On July 2, 2006, the Probo Koala called at Amsterdam port in the Netherlands to discharge the slops contained in the vessel's dedicated slops tanks. The vessel was en route to Paldiski, Estonia, to load gasoline for delivery to Lagos, Nigeria. Prior to arrival in Amsterdam, a fee had been agreed with a slops removal company, Amsterdam Port Services BV (APS). However, when approximately half of the slops had been discharged, APS increased the price by 3,000%. Trafigura's agents' view was this increase in price was provided without any credible justification. Discussions then followed between APS and the Amsterdam environmental authorities and Trafigura took no part in these discussions. APS then informed the ship's Master that the authorities had given permission for the slops previously removed to be returned to the vessel.

The Probo Koala departed Amsterdam on July 5, 2006 for Paldiski, Estonia, with the full knowledge and approval of the Dutch authorities. The vessel sailed to Paldiski, arriving there on July 9, 2006 where it unloaded approximately 3,300 metric tonnes of gasoline and loaded approximately 26,000 metric tonnes of unleaded gasoline from shore tanks at the Alexela Terminal. The Probo Koala departed Paldiski on July 13, 2006 on its pre-planned voyage. It arrived in Lagos on 30 July 2006. The purpose of the visit was to discharge unleaded gasoline to Pipelines Products Marketing Company Limited. This was completed on 16 August 2006 and the Probo Koala left Lagos on August 17, 2006.

It is normal for unloading to take this length of time in Lagos. it is also been informed that during the ship's stay in Lagos there were two offers to take the slops to shore. One involved offloading into an open barge, which the ship's Master refused. The second involved offloading into oil drums. The potential buyer planned to allow the slops to settle to reclaim useable oil and sell it on. The Master also refused the offer as he had concerns about the unlicensed import of hydrocarbons.

This unloading of the slops was overseen by a team from Ivorian Customs headed by Mr Yao Kuassi. The slops were discharged into waiting trucks under the supervision of the Port Authorities and Customs. Compagnie Tommy, or others, subsequently dumped the slops, untreated, in and around Abidjan. The evidence is so tainted that no one could reasonably conclude whether this was part of a pre-conceived plan or panic 'fly tipping' with the original purpose having been to sell on the slops as notorious 'black fuel'. Trafigura has publicly stated that Compagnie Tommy's conduct in dumping the slops in this manner was utterly reprehensible, illegal and a flagrant breach of Compagnie Tommy's licence and undertakings to them. It is understood that the slops contained a high percentage of hydrocarbons. It is also understood that these should have been capable of recovery even using the simplest method of leaving them in a container to allow the valuable parts and water and other items to separate naturally. On August 21, 2006, residents in and around Akouédo village complained of odours coming from the Akouédo site. On August 25, 2006, the Ivorian Government informed the Basel Secretariat of a pollution problem and requested assistance. The Ivorian Government further stated that the pollution problem was not confined to Akouédo but emanated from numerous locations in Abidjan. On September 3, 2006, reports of casualties were made. By September 11, 2006, the United Nations Disaster Assessment and Co-ordination, World Health Organisation, United Nations Office for the Co-ordination of Humanitarian Affairs and the Basel Secretariat were all present in Abidjan. These agencies were reacting to a series of reported deaths and over 3,000 people seeking medical care. On September 17, 2006, Tredi, the French company, commenced clean-up works at Akouédo. By October 14, 2006, 16 allegedly contaminated sites had apparently been identified and 13 had allegedly been de-polluted by Tredi.

It has been widely reported that as a major trading company in West Africa, Trafigura considered it had an economic and humanitarian responsibility to the region but not a legal responsibility for the event itself.

Komi, FSU

The Former Soviet Union (FSU) has over a million miles of gas and oil pipelines, many of them poorly maintained. Every year, up to one fifth of Russia's total oil production is lost partly through theft, but much of it through leakage. The company responsible for this 20-year-old pipeline, has a history of accidents caused by aging and corroded pipelines, they experience hundreds of leaks and ruptures each year, the ground is saturated with oil. Some of the oil has seeped into the water table. One of the main reasons for the large oil spills is the money made from the oil which drives officials to strain the antiquated infrastructure and to keep it moving despite breakdowns. October 1st 1994 the oil spill north of the town of Usinsk in the Komi Region of the FSU became the third largest oil spill in history. During the Cold War this area was top secret and no westerners were allowed near it. The pipeline just south of the Arctic Circle had been leaking since February 1994 but the oil was contained behind a dam. These are often constructed to contain spills, but heavy rains on October 1st broke down the dam and allowed the large lake of oil to spread over the tundra. Approx. 102,000m^3 of oil began to run over this highly sensitive area (Exxon Valdez was approx 35,000m^3). Some of this released oil flowed into the Kolva river; the Kolva river is a tributary of the Pechora river, which flows into the Barants sea. Most of the oil spread over an area of approx 187 km^2. at a time when weather conditions helped the containment and some was recovered the rest proceeded to freeze during the winter months. The main concern was the next spring thaw, which threatened to release much of the remaining oil into the rivers again. The Kolva and Usa river feeds into the Pechora river which contains large amounts of salmon and other valuable fish species. Teams built or reinforced enormous dams and constructed massive earthworks to hold oil laden floodwaters back. The structure of the top soil in this area differs greatly from site to site. In some places it is a peat bed with the mosses growing on the top, there is a permafrost which even during the summer is approx. One meter below the surface. In other areas the bed rock is very close to the surface with a fine layer of sand and the peat on top, in these areas the weight of the oil during the spring thaw slid the moss and sand off the rock, this meant that the oil now was mixed with this organic matter and could not be pumped back into the pipeline, so it was put into huge storage pits and set on fire, these pits burned for a couple of weeks they were filled again and the process repeated. As a part of the clean up operation over the next six months, the oil was deliberately set on fire in different areas in order to reduce the quantities that could spread as a result of the warmer temperatures. The smoke plume rose more than 8,000 feet and extended beyond the horizon some 40 miles away. With low temperatures, oil tends to persist for long periods of time because of the low evaporation rates. The frozen ground prevents the oil from seeping into it, and this allows it spread over large areas. In addition, disturbance to the thin layer of vegetation covering a frozen soil can precipitate a catastrophic and extensive erosion. The effects remain visible for many years. For example, it can take decades for a tree to grow one meter, and tyre tracks in tundra vegetation can remain for up to 100 years. Birch and Spruce trees growing in the area looked as if they were smothered with thick black shoe polish. Nearby lakes are resting grounds for migrating mallard ducks. There are many species that were likely to be affected by this spill. This region has one of the largest herds of domestic reindeer, estimated between 65,000-120,000 in the 1980s. Tundra environments are characterised by rich lichen communities which are susceptible to crude oil which they absorb very quickly. Reindeer are entirely dependent on lichen and are therefore were likely to be severely impacted. Commercial reindeer herding is one of the major industries in the Komi Republic. The Pechorskoye sea within the Berants sea holds some of the largest concentrations of white whales. There were also a number of birds and freshwater fish species that have been at risk.

Company was fined $600,000 for its pipeline spill. Although the company is unable to pay much of that sum because of its severe financial problems, it did give each resident of Ust-Usa 36,000 rubles about $7 in compensation. Greenpeace were given an invite to go to the area, they were horrified by what they saw and due to their reports of the damage done and so international money was asked for to accelerate the clean up. This case was handled by the Russian government in terms of cleaning up the oil. The European Bank for Reconstruction and Development lent the clean-up operation $25 million and the World Bank provided $100 million. From a sinical point of view most of it disappeared due to corruption and other powerful organisations. Greenpeace were not invited back probably because they had served their purpose. Damage like this all over Siberia. Just because someone happened to notice some oil floating down the river a couple of days ago, it suddenly makes the headlines, but the sad fact is it is not unusual. Local villagers have suffered for years from the effects of petroleum pollution from the many oil spills in the region. Most natives are worried about the fish living in the Kolva river. The river used to have lots of fish, now there are hardly any and when we cook them they smell bad, people here survive but they are worried about their future.

Baku, Azerbaijan

A brief history of the place will allow to understand that the population has been used to the smell of crude oil on the ground for over one hundred years so it's not new, it is common place. The existence of petroleum has been known since the 8th century. In the 10th century, an Arabian traveller reported that both white and black oil were being extracted naturally in Baku. By the 15th century oil for lamps was obtained from hand dug surface wells. First oil well was drilled in Baku in 1846. The Bolshevik revolution started in 1905 and ran through World War I. In 1918 Baku came under the control of Bolshevik's who inspired and condoned civil warfare in and around Baku, during this period the oil field were set on fire.

Large-scale oil development started in 1872, when the Russian imperial authorities auctioned the parcels of oil-rich land around Baku to private investors. Within a short period of time various European and American investors arrived in Baku, among them the drilling companies were the Nobel brothers and Rothschild to name but two, the industrial oil area, known as the Black City, which was established in the outskirts of the city. By the beginning of the 20th century the oil fields were the largest in the world. The revolution and civil unrest led to both Rothschild and the Nobel brothers leaving Baku. By 1900 the city had more than 3,000 oil wells of which 2,000 were producing oil at industrial levels.

The main export pipelines from here to the Black sea and Southern Turkey were constructed and paid for by the Foreign oil companies and are built to Western standards. Unfortunately the old original ones still continue to leak. If this area is ever to be cleaned up it will take Western money but what is the point when the pollution will just continue, it is part of the culture of the city, to smell crude oil is normal, the population has known nothing else for generations. In 2006 the world bank's representatives had talks with President Ilham Aliyev and other officials about a multi-million-dollar project to clean an area roughly the size of Malta.

The clean up would focus on oil-soaked areas in the Absheron peninsula, Azerbaijan's most densely populated region and location of the capital Baku. A clean-up of this size hasn't been undertaken anywhere. The latest news from Baku is that from a distance the contaminated area is beginning to look clean. Unfortunately on closer inspection lorry loads of earth is being tipped at the edges of the oiled areas and are being bulldozed over the oil.

Lebanon-Jiyye Oil Spill (July 2006)

On July 12, 2006 Israel declared war on Hezbollah in Lebanon. During conflicts it is normal to destroy enemy communication centres but on July 13 and 15, 2006 during the first days of the war Israeli forces bombed the Jiyyeh power plant, located on the coastline, 30 km South of Beirut, causing a major oil spill, two tanks at Jiyyeh caused approx. 25,000 m^3 to burn for more than three weeks smoke and vapours affected an area that is inhabited by approx. three million people. On the longer term, this may lead to increased respiratory and other health problems. Approx. 15,000 m^3 heavy fuel oil to spilled into the Sea. It became one of the largest environmental incidents in Mediterranean history. The wind was from the South West and Northerly current pushed the oil spill northwards along the coast of Lebanon. The affected area within Lebanon spread for more than 100 km of rocky shores and sandy beaches, marinas, ports, fishing harbours, and tourist resorts; from Jiyeh all the way up to the Syrian boarders. The oil entered Syria for approx 50 km. Sensitive fish spawning and nursery areas as well as valuable sea turtle nesting sites were in one of the affected areas.

The spill could have reached neighbouring countries such as Cyprus, Turkey and Greece depending on water currents and weather conditions. The impact of the oil spill caused tremendous negative environmental, social and economical impacts both for the short term and long term. It damaged marine ecosystems, damaged fishermen's livelihoods and rendered coastal areas lifeless. Heavy fuel oil, is among the most difficult oils to cleanup. Its viscous nature leads to prolonged persistence in the marine environment, such oils have the potential to cause widespread contamination of sensitive environmental and economic resources which will take many years to recover. The total direct economic cost of this oil spill has been estimated at more than 200 million dollars. The long term costs are not determined yet and are likely to be much more. Even a month after the attacks oil was still entering the sea. The oil settled deep into the sand, rocks and seabed. Cleanup operations could not start until the ceasefire was enforced. Delaying the start of cleanup operations made this spill harder to clean up. Despite the danger local NGOs, private sector and the Ministry of Environment started to cleanup certain sensitive and highly impacted areas. The delay caused the highly viscous heavy fuel to solidify; it emulsified with sea water, formed tar balls, lumps or emulsions, settled on the seabed and traveled further along the coast line. This makes clean up efforts and costs of clean up greater and mobility of experts and essential equipment nearly impossible. The absence of a pre-spill contingency plan made the job more difficult to allocate high and low priorities for the cleanup effort.

Local volunteers and a number of environmental activists formed an oil spill working group to follow on this issue and where among the first on the ground. Assessment operations and documentation of the damage started on the 17th of July covering the Lebanese coast from Beirut, northwards. Cleanup plans, scientific and economic research of the oil spill to determine the cost of the damage and how to minimise its impact as much as possible were carried out. The Lebanese Ministry of Environment, REMPEC (Regional Marine Pollution Emergency Response Center, Barcelona Convention, international NGOs and experts from around the World were contracted in. The cleanup had problem in mid 2007 due to lack of funds.

1991 Arabian Gulf

The Arabian Gulf, covers 233,100 km^2 is a kidney-shaped water body. It is approx. 917 km long with its greatest width being 338 km. The Tigris and Euphrates, two of the largest rivers the Middle East, merge together to form the Shatt-al-Arab waterway, the Gulf's main source of fresh water, flows primarily from Iraq into the northern end of the Gulf. Fresh water in the Gulf region comes from rain mainly in the winter months, which is also the lowest period of evaporation. The region's high summer temperatures, and the high evaporation rate make the Gulf water nearly one and a half times more saline than the oceans. The Gulf's counterclockwise current moves through the Strait of Hormuz along the Iranian coast past the Shatt-al-Arab then along the very shallow Saudi coastline. These shallow areas have been the resting place for oil spills. Anually approx 40,000 m^3 of oil is spilled in the Gulf. The Gulf's water circulation takes more than five years to return to Strait of Hormuz.

On January 21, 1991, a few days after the start of the air campaign against Iraq, the Iraqi military in Kuwait opened valves at the Sea Island oil terminal near Kuwait City and released massive quantities of crude oil into the

Gulf, as an act of environmental warfare (if we can't have the oil then neither can you). The oil moved southwards with the current and began to accumulate on the north coast of Saudi Arabia, where it endangered the fragile intertidal zones, mangrove forests and wildlife habitats such as bird feeding grounds and fish and shrimp nurseries. The first oil was spotted on January 24th the main source of oil appeared to be Kuwait's off-shore Sea Island terminal. The US Air Force bombed the terminal's shore side pipelines and manifold complex in an attempt to stop the oil flow. This bombing did not completely stop the flow and it was realised that other sources were contributing to the spill. Tankers near Mina Al Ahmadi, a damaged refinery south of Mina Al Ahmadi, the Iraqi Mina Al Bakr terminal, and tankers anchored north of Kuwait's Bubiyan Island. In early February 650 Kuwaiti oil wells were being set on fire when the ground war started. This caused problems with the satellite surveillance of the slick as they could not see thought the smoke. For the initial two weeks the winds were soft and from the southeast which slowed the oil from moving to the southwest and provided valuable time to prepare for it. Saudi governmental agencies together with oil companies from home and abroad started the difficult task of evaluating the amount and location of the oil using satellite imagery and mathematical models in order concentrate response resources. In February, 1992, an international team of scientists started a 100 day survey of the Area, mapping the shallow marine habitats around Abu Ali Island, a portion of the study area. The team found an asphalt pavement on the beaches of the island as well as along sections of the north of the island. The asphalt surface was approx. 0.2m thick. This pre-dated the 1991 War and indicated the long term effect on the Gulf. Saudi Arabia relies on desalinated sea water for its fresh water supply, sea water is also used for the cooling of electric power station and oil refineries. The object of the Iraqi exercise was to shut down all of these operations.

Fortunately the amount of boom and response personnel protected all of the sea water intakes by deflecting the oil past them. Abu Ali Island and Ad Daffi Bay which jut out into the Gulf approx. half way down the Saudi coast experienced the greatest pollution, with the main effect of the spill concentrated in the mangrove areas and shrimp grounds. Large numbers of marine birds, such as cormorants. The beaches around the entire bay shoreline were covered with oil and tar balls.

Many of the mangrove pneumatophore breathing roots became covered with oil resulting in the death of the trees. In some collection areas the oil was over a meter thick. Huge quantities of oil were removed and temporarily stored in huge pits built in the sand like this one, to give it scale the trucks on the right bottom are forty foot road tanks.

Much of the liquid oil was refined while large quantities were used, it was said to stabilize sand dunes in the desert as you can imagine there is no oil to be seen, a difficult task holding millions of tons of sand against the wind.

Chapter – 11

Anthropogenic Environmental Disasters

Anthropogenic is something that is caused or produced by humans. The human impact on the environment is also termed as *anthropogenic* impact on the environment. Such *anthropogenic* impact includes impacts on biophysical environments, biodiversity and other resources. One example of anthropogenic impact is the production of excessive greenhouse gasses by human actions. Described below are some *anthropogenic* environmental disasters, that is, environmental disasters which were caused by human actions or negligence.

Bhopal: The Union Carbide Gas Leak

3 December 1984 has become a day of mourning and bitter memories for the city of Bhopal, capital of the Madhya Pradesh state of India. This day is linked with an environmental disaster that is termed as the worst disaster to have ever occurred. On the midnight 2–3 December, a poisonous gas cloud escaped from the Union Carbide India Limited (UCIL) pesticide factory in Bhopal. The cloud contained 15 metric tons of methyl isocyanate

(MIC) gas, covering an area of more than 30 square miles. The gas leak killed at least 4,000 local residents instantly and caused health problems such as oedema for 50,000 to perhaps 500,000 people. These health problems killed around 15,000 more victims in the years that followed. Approximately 100,000 people still suffer from chronic diseases consequential to gas exposure. Research conducted by the BBC in 2004 pointed out that this pollution still causes people to fall ill, and ten more die every year.

The cause of the tragic Bhopal gas leak has been researched. Apparently, water ended up in MIC storage tanks in the UCIL factory, causing an exothermal reaction that released an amount of poisonous gas large enough to open the tanks' safety valves. Normally, scrubbers would intercept escaping gas, but these were temporarily out of order for repair. Research showed that factory personnel neglected a number of safety procedures. There were no valves to prevent water from entering the storage tanks. The cooling installation of the tanks and the flaring installation that might have flared the escaping gas were out of order.

Safety was very low in UCIL's Bhopal factory, compared to its other locations. The safety procedures were neglected because of budget cuts.

Union Carbide was accused of deliberate evasion of regular safety procedures. During lawsuits where victims demanded compensation, documents were presented which revealed that Union Carbide regularly used untested technology in the Bhopal factory. When the gas leak occurred, doctors were not informed of the nature of the gas. This prevented them from giving correct treatment to the gas leak victims and taking emergency measures.

Union Carbide CEO Warren Anderson was accused of culpable homicide. However, he did not appear in court and both the Indian and American governments did not take adequate measures to make sure this man was tried. This led to a series of protests organized by environmental organizations, such as Greenpeace.

Union Carbide denied responsibility for the accident on their website, stating that:

"The Bhopal plant was owned and operated by Union Carbide India, Limited (UCIL), an Indian company in which Union Carbide Corporation held just over half the stock. The other stockholders included Indian financial institutions and thousands of private investors in India. The plant was designed, built, and managed by UCIL using Indian consultants and workers."

About the cause of the accident, they claimed: "A thorough investigation was conducted by the engineering consulting firm Arthur D. Little. Its conclusion: the gas leak could only have been caused by deliberate sabotage. Someone purposely put water in the gas storage tank, causing a massive chemical reaction."

After a long procedure, eventually in February 1989, a settlement was reached between the Indian government and Union Carbide under which Union Carbide promised to pay 470 million dollars compensation. Only a very small part of this compensation was paid to survivors of the environmental disaster. Union Carbide states on its website that it paid the full settlement to the Indian government within 10 days time. In 2004, the Supreme Court forced the Indian government to pay the remaining 330 million dollars compensation to the victims and their families.

Union Carbide sold the Indian factory to a battery producer. In 2001 Dow Chemical Company took control of Union Carbide. These takeovers led to a discussion on responsibility for cleaning up the tonnes of poisonous waste that is still present in the environment consequential to the 1984 disaster. Environmental activists are trying to convince Dow Chemical Company to clean up this potential minefield of toxic chemicals. These could cause nervous system failure, liver and kidney disease and possibly cancer for many years to come.

Today, the UCIL location in Bhopal is still polluted with thousands of tonnes of toxic chemicals, such as hexachlorobenzene and mercury. These chemicals are stored in open barrels. Rainfall causes rinsing out of pollution to local drinking water sources. According to BBC research, some wells even contain up to 500 times the legal limit of these toxins. Local residents still suffer from a number of diseases, which appear to be very uncommon among people that do not live in the disaster area.

Seveso: Italian Dioxin Crisis

On midday of 10 July, 1976, an explosion occurred in a TCP (2,4,5-trichlorophenol) reactor in the ICMESA chemical company in Meda, Italy. A toxic cloud escaped into the atmosphere containing high concentrations of TCDD, a highly toxic form of dioxin. Downwind from the factory, the dioxin cloud polluted a densely populated area of six kilometres long and one kilometre wide, immediately killing many animals. A neighbouring municipality that was highly affected is called Seveso. The accident was named after this village. The dioxin cloud affected a total of 11 communities.

The media now mentions Seveso in line with major disasters such as Bhopal and Chernobyl, which have both become international symbols of industry-related diseases. However, the Seveso story is remarkably different when it comes to handling the pollution and the victims because earlier accidents had shown dioxin to be an extremely dangerous substance. Polluted areas were researched and the most severely polluted soils were excavated and treated elsewhere. Health effects caused as a consequence of the disaster were immediately recognized and victims were compensated. A long-term plan of health monitoring was put into operation. The Seveso victims suffered not only from a directly visible symptom known as chloracne but also from genetic impairments.

The Seveso accident and the immediate reaction of the authorities led to the introduction of European regulation for the prevention and control of heavy accidents involving toxic substances. This regulation is now known as the Seveso Directive. This Directive was a central guideline for European countries for managing industrial safety. The most remarkable feature of the Seveso accident was that local and regional authorities had no idea the plant was a source of risk. The factory existed for more than 30 years and the public had no idea of the possibility of an accident that occurred in 1976. The European Directive was created to prevent such ignorance in future and to enhance industrial safety. The Council of Ministers of The European Committee adopted the Directive in 1982. It obligates appropriate safety measures, and also public information on major industrial hazards, which is now known as the 'need to know' principle.

The 1952 London Smog Disaster

December 1952 caused over London the heaviest winter smog ever known to man. This smog lasted until March 1953. Light winds and a high moisture content created ideal conditions for smog formation. The unusual cold in London in the winter of 1952-1953 caused additional coal combustion, and many people travelled only by car, which caused the occurrence of a combination of black soot, sticky particles of tar and gaseous sulphur dioxide. This resulted in the heaviest winter smog over London.

Measurements suggested that the concentration of particulate matter in the air had reached 56 times its normal level. Sulphur dioxide concentration increased to seven times its peak level. The smoke particles trapped in the fog gave it a yellow-black colour. Sulphur dioxide reacted with substances in foggy droplets to form sulphuric acid, adding an intense form of acid rain to the process.

By the night of December 5, the smog was so dense that visibility dropped to only a few metres. Smog easily entered buildings, causing cinemas, theatres and stores to be closed. Transport became largely impossible. Motor vehicles were abandoned, trains were disrupted and airports were also closed. The smog killed approximately 12,000 people, mainly children, elderly people and people suffering from chronic respiratory or cardiac diseases. The number of deaths during the smog disaster was three or four times that on a normal day. They could be attributed to lung disease, tuberculosis and heart failure. Mortality from bronchitis and pneumonia increased more than seven-fold. Peaks of smoke and sulphur dioxide were in line with peaks in deaths. However, most deaths occurred because of breathing in acid aerosols, which irritates or inflames the bronchial tubes. Acidity was not measured, but estimates show that the pH probably fell to 2 during the peaks in the smog episode.

The highest death rate of 900 deaths per day was registered on 8–9 December during the smog episode. In some parts of London, death rates rose to nine times the normal number. Until spring, the death rate remained high at almost a thousand more deaths per week than expected in a normal winter.

This heavy pollution and its resulting death toll made people aware of the seriousness of air pollution. The London smog disaster resulted in the introduction of the first Clean Air Act in 1956.

Texaco Oil Exploration and Environmental Loss in Equador

In 1964, well-known US company Texaco Petroleum (now Chevron), discovered oil in the remote northern region of the Ecuadorian Amazon, known as the "Oriente." Texaco (Texpet) was minority partner in an exploration and production venture with Petroecuador, Ecuador's state-owned oil company. The production operation took place primarily on government lands. Roughly 1.7 billion barrels of crude oil were produced, with the Government of Ecuador (GOE) receiving 95 percent of the total financial proceeds accruing from oil exploaration.

The indigenous inhabitants of Oriente rainforest, including the Cofán, Siona, Secoya, Kichwa and Huaorani, lived traditional lifestyles largely untouched by modern civilization. The forests and rivers provided the physical and cultural subsistence base for their daily survival. They had little idea what to expect or how to prepare when oil workers moved into their backyard and founded the town of Lago Agrio, named for Texaco's birthplace of Sour Lake, Texas. The Ecuadorian government had similarly little idea what to expect; no one had ever successfully drilled for oil in the Amazon rainforest before. The government entrusted Texaco with more than a half-century's worth of experience, with employing modern oil practices and technology in the country's emerging oil patch. However, despite existing environmental laws, Texaco made deliberate, cost-cutting operational decisions that, for 28 years, resulted in an environmental catastrophe that experts have dubbed the "Rainforest Chernobyl."

Unlike the Exxon Valdez disaster that spilled over a billion gallons of crude during a one time cataclysmic event, Texaco's oil extraction system in Ecuador was designed, built, and operated on the cheap using substandard technology from the outset. This led to extreme, systematic pollution and exposure to toxins from multiple sources on a daily basis for almost three decades.

In a rainforest area roughly three times the size of Manhattan, Texaco carved out 350 oil wells, and upon leaving the country in 1992, left behind some 1,000 open toxic waste pits. Many of these pits leak into the water table or overflow in heavy rains, polluting rivers and streams that 30,000 people depend on for drinking, cooking, bathing and fishing. Texaco also dumped more than 18 billion gallons of toxic and highly saline "formation waters," a byproduct of the drilling process, into the rivers of the Oriente. At the height of Texaco's operations, the company was dumping an estimated 4 million gallons of formation waters per day – a practice outlawed in major US oil-producing states like Louisiana, Texas and California decades before the company began operations in Ecuador in 1967. By handling its toxic waste in Ecuador in ways that were illegal in its home country, Texaco saved an estimated $3 per barrel of oil produced.

Oil Exploration Trouble Nigeria

Nigeria is the land of over 250 tribes. The oil-rich Niger Delta belongs to 4 or 5 tribes but the Nigerian government is made up of different ones. The money earned by the government goes to places like Switzerland and little or in truth nothing returns to the Niger Delta region. The people get some money from Shell by drilling holes in the pipelines or opening valves, sometimes even using explosives to cause a pollution problem for which they then require compensation. It is quite a common event for someone to hole a gasoline line then everyone is in line with anything that will hold liquid. From time to time there are huge fires during these incidents and it is not uncommon for hundreds of people to die or be badly burnt. The gas flares in the delta region are usually in big pits; the locals cook cassava part of the local diet here. They usually have black spots made by oil that passes the flare.

In recent years a various ethnic militia groups calling themselves the Movement for the Emancipation of the Niger Delta (MEND), Niger Delta People's Volunteer Force (NDPVF) and Niger Delta Vigilante (NDV) have been taking oil workers hostage and damaging the oil infrastructure, such as terminals, pipeline, valves and rigs. As with all of the world's terrorist organisations, recruiting people, raising money and buying arms for a cause is not difficult for these ethnic militia groups. Their arms in many cases are better than the army and police have. There are few negotiations or steps taken for these groups to stop. But kidnappings and damage to the oil infrastructure and the environment continue. This of course will continue until the Delta region gets something for what they think is their oil or the government stops being corrupt.

Brazil: The 1998 Roraima Wildfires

In 1998, raging wildfires brought on by unimaginable droughts swept the northern Brazilian state Roraima. The fires took place on its savannahs, grassland and deciduous forests. Hundreds of people were killed in the fires and one of the planet's most primitive peoples, the Yanomami Indians, were threatened.

According to researchers, Roraima wildfires were the worst in the history of the Amazon region.The first fires were reportedly started to clear forests for agricultural land. Farmers in Brazil often burn parts of forest to gain fertile farmland. But droughts caused Roraima fires to turn into wildfires and linger rather than burn out.

Burning fronts were as wide as 5,6 kilometres. News reports and local residents described flames and smoke reaching as high as 30 m into the air. The smoke blocked the sun and blackened the sky. The fires were completely out of control and spread rapidly as a result of persistent winds, eventually destroying more than 34.000 km^2 of forest.

The rapidly spreading fires ruined most of the province's agricultural land and killed livestock and wild animals in very large numbers. Incalculable damage was done to the environment. According to some environmental institutes, it would take more than 100 years for the forests to recover. Estimates stated that 12-16% of the vegetation in the province was destroyed.

One of the most prominent consequences of the wildfires is atmospheric pollution. In 1998 this caused many people to experience respiratory disease and other symptoms. It is estimated that the number of people hospitalised with breathing problems increased up to 3.2 percent during the burning period in Brazil in comparison to earlier years. This severely increased the expenditure in the health sector.

Other effects of Brazilian wildfires on society were:

- Disruption of air and ground transportation services by smoke
- Potential contributions to global climate change by greenhouse gas production
- Water quality reduction
- Interruptions in electrical energy supply
- Deaths and property loss
- Biodiversity loss
- Problems for commercial plantations

During the Roraima wildfires, outside sources were not mobilised quickly enough to stop the fires from spreading. There was no external communication between firefighting organizations. There was a severe lack of adequate firefighting equipment and of air support. The fire fighters were often not adequately trained to work in the circumstances created by the Brazilian wildfires. Farmers kept on clearing forest by combustion even after warnings not to do so by the government. Brazilian law now prohibits burning during the dry season.

Other Known Wildfires

Wildfires have occurred all over the world, particularly in forest regions.

Some major incidents of wildfires are listed below:

- **1871** – Forest fires in Wisconsin and Michigan destroyed 1.7 million hectares and killed 2,200 people.
- **1915** – Great Siberian fire destroyed 1 million km^2 of land. Huge amounts of smoke blocked incoming solar radiation, decreasing global temperatures.
- **1980** – Canada forest fires destroyed 4.8 million hectares.
- **1983** – Ash fires in South Australia and Victoria destroyed over 0.5 million hectares, including 24 towns, forest and pasture. The fires killed 76 people and injured another 3,500.
- **1988** – Yellowstone National Park fires, US, destroyed 650,000 hectares and cost 120 million dollars.
- **1991** – Forest fires in Oakland and Berkley, California killed 25 people, injured 150, destroyed 2,886 homes, and caused some 1.5 billion dollars in damage
- **1998** – Indonesia fires: smoke travelled for thousands of miles, affecting millions of people.
- **2000** – Cerro Grande fires in New Mexico destroyed at least 235 homes and burned some 20,230 hectares.

Chapter – 12

Disaster Management

Disaster management is the generic name of an interdisciplinary field dealing with the strategic organizational management processes used to protect critical assets of an organization from hazard risks that can cause disasters or catastrophes, and to ensure their continuance within their planned lifetime. Assets are categorized as either living things, non-living things, cultural or economic. Hazards are categorized by their cause, either natural or human-made. The entire strategic management process is divided into four fields which normally deal with risk reduction, preparing resources to respond to the hazard, responding to the actual damage caused by the hazard and limiting further damage (e.g., emergency evacuation, quarantine, mass decontamination, etc.), and returning as close as possible to the state before the hazard incident. Disaster management is undertaken in both the public and private sectors, sharing the same processes, but with different focus. Disaster management is a strategic process, and not a tactical process, thus it usually resides at the Executive level in an organization. It normally has no direct power, but serves as an advisory or coordinating function to ensure that all parts of an organization are focused on the common goal. Effective disaster management relies on a thorough integration of emergency plans at all levels of the organization, and an understanding that the lowest levels of the organization are responsible for managing the emergency and getting additional resources and assistance from the upper levels. The most senior person in the organization administering disaster management is normally called an emergency manager, or a derived form based upon the term used in the field (e.g. business continuity manager).

The fields that are covered by the definition of disaster management include:

- Civil defence used during the Cold War, focusing on protection from nuclear attack
- Civil protection widely used in the European Union
- Crisis management emphasizes the political and security dimension rather than measure to satisfy the immediate needs of the civilian population.
- Disaster risk reduction focuses on the mitigation and preparedness aspects of the emergency cycle.
- Homeland security focusing on preventing terrorism.
- Business continuity and business continuity planning focuses on ensuring a continuous upward trend of income.
- Continuity of government

The nature of disaster management depends on local economic and social conditions. Some disaster relief experts such as Fred Cuny have stated that in a sense the only real disasters are economic. Experts have long noted that the cycle of Emergency disaster management must include long-term work on infrastructure, public awareness, and even human justice issues. The process of emergency management involves four phases: mitigation, preparedness, response, and recovery. The FEMA (Federal Emergency Management Agency) of the USA has adopted the terms "resilience" and "prevention" as part of the paradigm of emergency management (EM). The two terms do not fit easily as separate phases. Prevention by definition is 100% mitigation. Resilience describes the goal of the four phases: an ability to recover from or adjust easily to misfortune or change.

Principles of Emergency Disaster Management

In 2007, Dr. Wayne Blanchard of FEMA's Emergency Management Higher Education Project, at the direction of Dr. Cortez Lawrence, Superintendent of FEMA's Emergency Management Institute, convened a working group of emergency management practitioners and academics to consider principles of emergency management. This project was prompted by the realization that while numerous books, articles and papers referred to "principles of emergency management," nowhere in the vast array of literature on the subject was there an agreed-upon definition of what these principles were. The group agreed on eight principles that will be used to guide the development of a doctrine of emergency management. The following summary lists these eight principles and provides a brief description of each.

1. Comprehensive – Emergency managers consider and take into account all hazards, all phases, all stakeholders and all impacts relevant to disasters.
2. Progressive – Emergency managers anticipate future disasters and take preventive and preparatory measures to build disaster-resistant and disaster-resilient communities.
3. Risk-driven – Emergency managers use sound risk management principles (hazard identification, risk analysis, and impact analysis) in assigning priorities and resources.

4. Integrated – Emergency managers ensure unity of effort among all levels of government and all elements of a community.
5. Collaborative – Emergency managers create and sustain broad and sincere relationships among individuals and organizations to encourage trust, advocate a team atmosphere, build consensus, and facilitate communication.
6. Coordinated – Emergency managers synchronize the activities of all relevant stakeholders to achieve a common purpose.
7. Flexible – Emergency managers use creative and innovative approaches in solving disaster challenges.
8. Professional – Emergency managers value a science and knowledge-based approach, based on education, training, experience, ethical practice, public stewardship and continuous improvement.

Mitigation

Mitigation efforts are attempts to prevent hazards from developing into disasters altogether or to reduce the effects of disasters. The mitigation phase differs from the other phases in that it focuses on long-term measures for reducing or eliminating risk. The implementation of mitigation strategies is part of the recovery process if applied after a disaster. Mitigation measures can be structural or non-structural. Structural measures use technological solutions like flood levees. Non-structural measures include legislation, land-use planning (e.g. designation of nonessential land like parks to be used as flood zones), and insurance. Mitigation is the most cost-efficient method for reducing the effect of hazards although not always the most suitable. Mitigation includes providing regulations regarding evacuation, sanctions against those who refuse to obey the regulations (such as mandatory evacuations), and communication of risks to the public.

Some structural mitigation measures may harm the ecosystem. A precursor to mitigation is the identification of risks. Physical risk assessment refers to identifying and evaluating hazards. The hazard-specific risk combines a hazard's probability and effects. The equation states that the hazard multiplied by the population's vulnerability to that hazard produces a risk catastrophe modeling. The higher the risk the more urgent the targeting of vulnerabilities to the hazard by mitigation and preparedness. If, however, there is no vulnerability then there will be no risk, for example, an earthquake occurring in a desert where nobody lives.

Personal mitigation is mainly about knowing and avoiding unnecessary risks. This includes an assessment of possible risks to personal/family health and to personal property. One example of personal mitigation would be to avoid buying property that is exposed to hazards, for example, in a flood plain, in areas of subsidence or landslides. Home owners may not be aware of a property being exposed to a hazard until it strikes. However, specialists can be hired to conduct risk identification and assessment surveys. Purchase of insurance covering the most prominent identified risks is a common measure.

Mitigation involves structural and non-structural measures taken to limit the impact of disasters.

Structural Mitigation: This involves proper layout of building, particularly to make it resistant to disasters.

Non Structural Mitigation: This involves measures taken other than improving the structure of building.

Personal structural mitigation in earthquake-prone areas includes installation of an earthquake valve to instantly shut off the natural gas supply to a property, seismic retrofits of property and the securing of items inside a building to enhance household seismic safety. The latter may include the mounting of furniture, refrigerators, water heaters and breakables to the walls, and the addition of cabinet latches. In flood-prone areas houses can be built on poles/stilts, as in much of southern Asia. In areas prone to prolonged electricity black-outs, installation of a generator would be an example of an optimal structural mitigation measure. The construction of storm cellars and fallout shelters are further examples of personal mitigative actions.

Preparedness

Personal preparedness focuses on preparing equipment and procedures for use when a disaster occurs, that is, planning. Preparedness measures can take many forms including construction of shelters, installation of warning devices, creation of back-up life-line services (e.g. power, water and sewage), and rehearsing evacuation plans. Two simple measures can help prepare the individual for sitting out the event or evacuating, as necessary. For evacuation, a disaster supplies kit may be prepared and for sheltering purposes a stockpile of supplies may be created. The preparation of a survival kit such as a "72-hour kit", is often advocated by authorities. These kits may include food, medicine, flashlights, candles and money. Also, putting valuable items in safe area is recommended.

Preparedness is a continuous cycle of planning, organizing, training, equipping, exercising, evaluation and improvement activities to ensure effective coordination and enhancement of capabilities to prevent, protect against, respond to, recover from, and mitigate the effects of natural disasters, acts of terrorism, and other man-made disasters. Another aspect of preparedness is casualty prediction, that is, the study of how many deaths or injuries to expect for a given kind of event. This gives planners an idea of what resources need to be in place to respond to a particular kind of event.

In the preparedness phase, emergency managers develop plans of action to manage and counter their risks and take action to build the necessary capabilities needed to implement such plans. Common preparedness measures include:

1. Communication plans with easily understandable terminology and methods.
2. Proper maintenance and training of emergency services, including mass human resources such as community emergency response teams.
3. Development and exercise of emergency population warning methods combined with emergency shelters and evacuation plans.
4. Stockpiling, inventory, and maintaining disaster supplies and equipment
5. Developing organizations of trained volunteers among civilian populations. Professional emergency workers are rapidly overwhelmed in mass emergencies. So trained, organized, responsible volunteers are extremely valuable. Organizations like Community Emergency Response Teams and the Red Cross are ready sources of trained volunteers. The latter's emergency management system has gotten high ratings from both California, and the Federal Emergency Management Agency (FEMA).

Emergency managers in the planning phase should be flexible, and all-encompassing. They should carefully recognize the risks and exposures of their respective regions and employ unconventional and atypical means of support. Depending on the region — municipal or private sector — emergency services can rapidly be depleted and heavily taxed. Non-governmental organizations (NGOs) that offer desired resources should be identified early in planning stages, and they should practice their emergency drills with regularity. NGO help could be in the form of transportation of displaced homeowners to be conducted by local school district buses, evacuation of flood victims to be performed by mutual aide agreements between fire departments and rescue squads.

Response

Nine common objectives of disaster response are:

1. To save life
2. To prevent escalation of the disaster
3. To relieve suffering
4. To safeguard the environment
5. To protect property
6. To facilitate criminal investigation and judicial, public, technical, or other inquiries
7. To inform the public
8. To promote self-help and recovery
9. To restore normalcy as soon as possible

The response phase of an emergency may commence with search and rescue but in all cases the focus will quickly turn to fulfilling the basic humanitarian needs of the affected population. This assistance may be provided by national or international agencies and organisations. Effective coordination of disaster assistance is often crucial, particularly when many organizations respond and local emergency management agency (LEMA) capacity has been exceeded by the demand or diminished by the disaster itself.

On a personal level the response can take the shape either of a shelter-in-place or an evacuation. In a shelter-in-place scenario, a family would be prepared to fend for themselves in their home for many days without any form of outside support. In an evacuation, a family leaves the area by automobile or other mode of transportation, taking with them the maximum amount of supplies they can carry, possibly including a tent for shelter. If mechanical transportation is not available, evacuation on foot would ideally include carrying at least three days of supplies and rain-tight bedding, a tarpaulin and a bedroll of blankets being the minimum.

The response includes the mobilization of the necessary emergency services and first responders in the disaster area. This is likely to include a first wave of core emergency services, such as firefighters, police and ambulance crews. When conducted as a military operation, it is termed Disaster Relief Operation (DRO) and can be a follow-up to a non-combatant evacuation operation (NEO). They may be supported by a number of secondary emergency services, such as specialist rescue teams. A well-rehearsed emergency plan developed as part of the preparedness phase enables efficient coordination of rescue. Where required, search and rescue efforts commence at an early stage. Depending on injuries sustained by the victim, outside temperature, and victim access to air and water, the vast majority of those affected by a disaster will die within 72 hours after impact. Organizational response to any significant disaster – natural or terrorist-borne — is based on existing emergency management organizational systems and processes: the Federal Response Plan (FRP) and the Incident Command System (ICS). These systems are solidified through the principles of Unified Command (UC) and Mutual Aid (MA) There is a need for both discipline (structure, doctrine and process) and agility (creativity, improvisation and adaptability) in responding to a disaster. Combining that with the need to onboard and build a high functioning leadership team quickly to coordinate and manage efforts as they grow beyond first responders indicates the need for a leader and his or her team to craft and implement a disciplined, iterative set of response plans. This allows the team to move forward with coordinated, disciplined responses that are vaguely right and adapt to new information and changing circumstances along the way.

Recovery

The aim of the recovery phase is to restore the affected area to its previous state. It differs from the response phase in its focus; recovery efforts are concerned with issues and decisions that must be made after immediate needs are addressed. Recovery efforts are primarily concerned with actions that involve rebuilding destroyed property, re-employment, and the repair of other essential infrastructure. Efforts should be made to 'build back better', aiming to reduce the pre-disaster risks inherent in the community and infrastructure. An important aspect of effective recovery efforts is taking advantage of a 'window of opportunity' for the implementation of mitigative measures that might otherwise be unpopular. Citizens of the affected area are more likely to accept more mitigative changes when a recent disaster is in fresh memory.

The recovery phase starts after the immediate threat to human life has subsided. During reconstruction it is recommended to consider the location or construction material of the property. The most extreme home confinement scenarios include war, famine and severe epidemics and may last a year or more. Then recovery will take place inside the home. Planners for these events usually buy bulk foods and appropriate storage and preparation equipment, and eat the food as part of normal life. A simple balanced diet can be constructed from vitamin pills, whole-meal wheat, beans, dried milk, corn, and cooking oil. One should add vegetables, fruits, spices and meats, both prepared and fresh-gardened, when possible.

Emergency managers are trained in a wide variety of disciplines that support them throughout the emergency life-cycle. Professional emergency managers can focus on government and community preparedness (Continuity of Operations/Continuity of Government Planning), or private business preparedness (Business Continuity Management Planning). Training is provided by local, state, federal and private organizations and ranges from public information and media relations to high-level incident command and tactical skills such as studying a terrorist bombing site or controlling an emergency scene. In the past, the field of emergency management has been populated mostly by people with a military or first responder background. Currently, the population in the field has become more diverse, with many experts coming from a variety of backgrounds without military or first responder history. Educational opportunities are increasing for those seeking undergraduate and graduate degrees in emergency management or a related field. There are over 180 schools in the US with emergency management-related programs, but only one doctoral program specifically in emergency management. Professional certifications such as Certified Emergency Manager (CEM) and Certified Business Continuity Professional (CBCP) are becoming more common as the need for high professional standards is recognized by the emergency management community.

Tools

The joint efforts of professional associations and cultural heritage institutions have resulted in the development of a variety of tools to assist professionals in preparing disaster and recovery plans. In many cases, these tools are made available to external users. Also frequently available on websites are plan templates created by existing organizations, which may be helpful to any committee or group preparing a disaster plan or updating an existing plan. While each organization will need to formulate plans and tools which meet their own specific needs, there are some examples of such tools that might represent useful starting points in the planning process. In 2009, the US Agency for International Development created a web-based tool for estimating populations impacted by disasters. Called Population Explorer, the tool uses Landscan population data, developed by Oak Ridge National Laboratory, to distribute population at a resolution 1 km^2 for all countries in the world. Used by USAID's FEWS NET Project to estimate populations vulnerable and or impacted by food insecurity, Population Explorer is gaining wide use in a range of emergency analysis and response actions, including estimating populations impacted by floods in Central America and a Pacific Ocean Tsunami event in 2009.

In 2007, a checklist for veterinarians pondering participation in emergency response was published. It had two sections of questions for a professional to ask himself/herself before assisting with an emergency. The two sections of questions are:

Absolute requirements for participation: Have I chosen to participate? Have I taken ICS training? Have I taken other required background courses? Have I made arrangements with my practice to deploy? Have I made arrangements with my family?

Incident Participation: Have I been invited to participate? Are my skill sets a match for the mission? Can I access just-in-time training to refresh skills or acquire needed new skills? Is this a self-support mission? Do I have supplies needed for three to five days of self support?

In recent years the continuity feature of emergency management has resulted in a new concept, Emergency Management Information Systems (EMIS). For continuity and interoperability between emergency management stakeholders, EMIS supports the emergency management process by providing an infrastructure that integrates emergency plans at all levels of government and non-government involvement and by utilizing the management of all related resources (including human and other resources) for all four phases of emergencies. In the healthcare field, hospitals utilize HICS (Hospital Incident Command System) which provides structure and organization in a clearly defined chain of command with a set responsibilities for each division.

Practitioners in emergency management (disaster preparedness) come from an increasing variety of backgrounds as the field matures. Professionals from memory institutions (e.g. museums, historical societies, libraries, and archives) are dedicated to preserving cultural heritage — objects and records contained in their collections. This has been an increasingly major component within these fields as a result of the heightened awareness following the September 11 attacks in 2001, the hurricanes in 2005, and the collapse of the Cologne Archives. To increase the opportunity for a successful recovery of valuable records, a well-established and thoroughly tested plan must be developed. This plan must not be overly complex, but rather emphasize simplicity in order to aid in response and recovery. As an example of the simplicity, employees should perform similar tasks in the response and recovery phase that they perform under normal conditions. It should also include mitigation strategies such as the installation of sprinklers within the institution. This task requires the cooperation of a well-organized committee led by an experienced chairperson. Professional associations schedule regular workshops and hold focus sessions at annual conferences to keep individuals up to date with tools and resources in practice in order to minimize risk and maximize recovery.

International Organizations Involved in Disaster Management

United Nations

Within the United Nations system, responsibility for emergency response rests with the Resident Coordinator within the affected country. However, in practice, international response will be coordinated, if requested by the affected country's government, by the UN Office for the Coordination of Humanitarian Affairs (UN-OCHA) by deploying a UN Disaster Assessment and Coordination (UNDAC) team.

World Bank

Since 1980, the World Bank has approved more than 500 operations related to disaster management, amounting to more than US$40 billion. These include post-disaster reconstruction projects as well as projects with components aimed at preventing and mitigating disaster impacts, in countries such as Argentina, Bangladesh, Colombia, Haiti, India, Mexico, Turkey and Vietnam to name only a few. Common areas of focus for prevention and mitigation projects include forest fire prevention measures, such as early warning measures and education campaigns to discourage farmers from slash and burn agriculture that ignites forest fires; early-warning systems for hurricanes; flood prevention mechanisms, ranging from shore protection and terracing in rural areas to adaptation of production; and earthquake-prone construction. In a joint venture with Columbia University under the umbrella of the ProVention Consortium, the World Bank has established a Global Risk Analysis of Natural Disaster Hotspots. In June 2006, the World Bank established the Global Facility for Disaster Reduction and Recovery (GFDRR), a longer term partnership with other aid donors to reduce disaster losses by mainstreaming disaster risk reduction in development, in support of the Hyogo

Framework of Action. The facility helps developing countries fund development projects and programs that enhance local capacities for disaster prevention and emergency preparedness.

European Union

Since 2001, the EU adopted Community Mechanism for Civil Protection which started to play a significant role on the global scene. The Mechanism's main role is to facilitate co-operation in civil protection assistance interventions in the event of major emergencies which may require urgent response actions. This applies also to situations where there may be an imminent threat of such major emergencies. The heart of the Mechanism is the Monitoring and Information Centre (MIC). It is part of Directorate-General for Humanitarian Aid & Civil Protection of the European Commission and accessible 24 hours a day. It gives countries access to a platform — a one-stop-shop of civil protection means that is available among all the participating states. Any country inside or outside the Union affected by a major disaster can make an appeal for assistance through the MIC. It acts as a communication hub at headquarters level between participating states, the affected country and despatched field experts. It also provides useful and updated information on the actual status of an ongoing emergency.

International Recovery Platform

The International Recovery Platform (IRP) was conceived at the World Conference on Disaster Reduction (WCDR) in Kobe, Hyogo, Japan in January 2005. As a thematic platform of the International Strategy for Disaster Reduction (ISDR) system, IRP is a key pillar for the implementation of the Hyogo Framework for Action (HFA) 2005–2015: Building the Resilience of Nations and Communities to Disasters, a global plan for disaster risk reduction for the decade adopted by 168 governments at the WCDR. The key role of IRP is to identify gaps and constraints experienced in post-disaster recovery and to serve as a catalyst for the development of tools, resources, and capacity for resilient recovery. IRP aims to be an international source of knowledge on good recovery practice.

International Association of Emergency Managers

The International Association of Emergency Managers (IAEM) is a non-profit educational organization dedicated to promoting the goals of saving lives and protecting property during emergencies and disasters. The mission of IAEM is to serve its members by providing information, networking and professional opportunities, and to advance the emergency management profession. It currently has seven councils around the world: Asia, Canada, Europe, International, Oceania, Student and the USA. IAEM also administers the following programme on behalf of the profession: Certified Emergency Manager(CEM) Scholarship Program. The Air Force Emergency Management Association, loosely affiliated by membership with the IAEM, provides emergency management information and networking.

Red Cross/Red Crescent

National Red Cross/Red Crescent societies often have pivotal roles in responding to emergencies. Additionally, the International Federation of Red Cross and Red Crescent Societies (IFRC, or "The Federation") may deploy assessment teams (e.g. Field Assessment and Coordination Team — FACT) to the affected country if requested by the national Red Cross or Red Crescent Society. After having assessed the needs Emergency Response Units (ERUs) may be deployed to the affected country or region. They are specialized in the response component of the emergency management framework.

National Organizations Involved in Disaster Management

Australia

The key federal coordinating and advisory body for emergency management in Australia is Emergency Management Australia (EMA). Each of the five states and two territories of Australia has its own State emergency service. The emergency call service provides a national 000 emergency telephone number to contact state police, fire and ambulance services. Arrangements are in place for state and federal cooperation.

Canada

Public Safety Canada is Canada's national emergency management agency. Each province is required to have legislation in place for dealing with emergencies, as well as establish their own emergency management agencies, typically called an "Emergency Measures Organization" (EMO), which functions as the primary liaison with the municipal and federal level.

Public Safety Canada coordinates and supports the efforts of federal organizations ensuring national security and the safety of Canadians. They also work with other levels of government, first responders, community groups, private sector (operators of critical infrastructure) and other nations.

Public Safety Canada's work is based on a wide range of policies and legislation through the Public Safety and Emergency Preparedness Act which defines the powers, duties and functions of Public Safety Canada. Other acts are specific to fields such as corrections, emergency management, law enforcement and national security.

Germany

In Germany, the Federal Government controls the German Katastrophenschutz (disaster relief) and Zivilschutz (civil protection) programmes. The local units of German fire department and the Technisches Hilfswerk (Federal Agency for Technical Relief, THW) are part of these programmes. The German Armed Forces (Bundeswehr), the German Federal Police and the 16 state police forces (Länderpolizei) all have been deployed for disaster relief operations. Besides the German Red Cross, humanitarian help is dispensed by the Johanniter-Unfallhilfe, the German equivalent of the St. John Ambulance, the Malteser-Hilfsdienst, the Arbeiter-Samariter-Bund, and other private organizations. As of 2006, there is a joint course at the University of Bonn leading to the degree Master in Disaster Prevention and Risk Governance.

India

The role of emergency management organisation is played by the National Disaster Management Authority of India, a government agency subordinate to the Ministry of Home Affairs. In recent years there has been a shift in emphasis from response and recovery to strategic risk management and reduction, and from a government-centred approach to decentralized community participation. The Ministry of Science and Technology supports an internal agency that facilitates research by bringing the academic knowledge and expertise of earth scientists to emergency management.

A group representing a public/private partnership has recently been formed by the Government of India. It is funded primarily by a large India-based computer company and is aimed at improving the general response of communities to emergencies in addition to those incidents which might be described as disasters. Some of the groups' early efforts involve provision of emergency management training for first responders (a first in India), creation of a single emergency telèphone number, and establishment of standards for EMS staff, equipment, and training. It operates in three states though efforts are being made in making this a nation-wide effective group.

The Netherlands

In the Netherlands, the Ministry of the Interior and Kingdom Relations is responsible for emergency preparedness and emergency management on national level and operates a national crisis centre (NCC). The country is divided into 25 safety regions (veiligheidsregio). Each safety region is covered by three services: police, fire and ambulance. All regions operate according to the Coordinated Regional Incident Management System. Other services such as the Ministry of Defence, waterboard(s) andRijkswaterstaat can have an active role in the emergency management process.

New Zealand

In New Zealand, the responsibility for emergency management moves from local to national depending on the nature of the emergency or risk reduction programme. A severe storm may be manageable within a particular area, whereas a national public education campaign will be directed by the central government. Within each region, local governments are unified into 16 Civil Defence Emergency Management Groups (CDEMGs). Every CDEMG is responsible for ensuring that local emergency management is as robust as possible. As local arrangements are overwhelmed by an emergency, pre-existing mutual-support arrangements are activated. As warranted, the central government has the authority to coordinate the response through the National Crisis Management Centre

(NCMC), operated by the Ministry of Civil Defence and Emergency Management (MCDEM). These structures are defined by regulation and best explained in The Guide to the National Civil Defence Emergency Management Plan 2006, roughly equivalent to the US Federal Emergency Management Agency's National Response Framework.

New Zealand uses a terminology for emergency management that is unique in the English-speaking world. Some terms of this terminology are described below:

4Rs is a term used to describe the emergency management cycle locally. The four phases of this cycle are known as:

- Reduction = Mitigation
- Readiness = Preparedness
- Response
- Recovery

Emergency management is rarely used locally; many government publications retain usage of the term civil defence. For example, the Minister of Civil Defence is responsible for the central government's emergency management agency, MCDEM.

Civil Defence Emergency Management is a term in its own right. Often abbreviated as CDEM, it is defined by statute as the application of knowledge to prevent harm from disasters.

Disaster very rarely appears in official publications. In a New Zealand context, the terms emergency and incident usually appear when speaking about disasters in general. When describing an emergency that has had a response from the authorities, the term event is also used. For example, publications refer to the "Canterbury Snow Event 2002"

Russia

In Russia the Ministry of Emergency Situations (EMERCOM) is engaged in fire fighting, civil defence, search and rescue, including rescue services after natural and human-made disasters.

United Kingdom

The United Kingdom adjusted its focus on emergency management following the 2000 UK fuel protests, severe flooding in the same year and the 2001 United Kingdom foot-and-mouth crisis. This resulted in the creation of the Civil Contingencies Act 2004 (CCA) which defined some organisations as Category 1 and 2 Responders. These responders have responsibilities under the legislation regarding emergency preparedness and response. The CCA is managed by the Civil Contingencies Secretariat through Regional Resilience Forums and at the local authority level. Disaster management training is generally conducted at the local level by the organisations involved in any response. This is consolidated through professional courses that can be undertaken at the Emergency Planning College. Furthemore, diplomas, undergraduate and postgraduate qualifications can be gained throughout the country — the first course of this type was carried out by Coventry University in 1994. The Institute of Emergency Management is a charity, established in 1996, providing consulting services for the government, media and commercial sectors. The Professional Society for Emergency Planners is the Emergency Planning Society. One of the largest emergency exercises in the UK was carried out on 20 May, 2007 near Belfast, Northern Ireland, and involved the scenario of a plane crash landing at Belfast International Airport. Staff from five hospitals and three airports participated in the drill, and almost 150 international observers assessed its effectiveness.

United States

Under the Department of Homeland Security (DHS), the Federal Emergency Management Agency (FEMA) is lead agency for emergency management. The HAZUS software package developed by FEMA is central in the risk assessment process in the country. The United States and its territories are covered by one of ten regions for FEMA's emergency management purposes. Tribal, state, county and local governments develop emergency management programmes/departments and operate hierarchically within each region. Emergencies are managed at the most-local level possible, utilizing mutual aid agreements with adjacent jurisdictions. If the emergency is terrorist related or if declared an 'Incident of National Significance', the Secretary of Homeland Security will initiate the National Response Framework (NRF). Under this plan, the involvement of federal resources will be made possible, integrating in with the local, county, state, or tribal entities. Management will continue to be handled at the lowest possible level utilizing the National Incident Management System (NIMS).

The Citizen Corps is an organization of volunteer service programmes, administered locally and coordinated nationally by DHS, which seeks to mitigate disaster and prepare the population for emergency response through public education, training, and outreach. Community Emergency Response Teams are a Citizen Corps programme focused on disaster preparedness and teaching basic disaster response skills. These volunteer teams are utilized to provide emergency support when disaster overwhelms the conventional emergency services. The US Congress established the Center for Excellence in Disaster Management and Humanitarian Assistance (COE) as the principal agency to promote disaster preparedness and societal resiliency in the Asia-Pacific region. As part of its mandate, COE facilitates education and training in disaster preparedness, consequence management and health security to develop domestic, foreign and international capability and capacity.

Seismic Retrofitting in India (Latur to Kashmir)

Seismic retrofitting for reduction of vulnerability of a structure is a relatively new concept in India. It was only after the Latur earthquake of 1993 that retrofitting was taken up on a substantial scale as part of the earthquake rehabilitation programme under which many public buildings were retrofitted. The quantum got substantially increased in the aftermath of 2001 Kachch Earthquake.

In India, retrofitting as an option, a technique, a profession or a business is still in its infancy. This is manifested by five indicators — (a) A delivery system for retrofitting does not exist; (b) Official schedule of rates (SOR) of any government agency does not include seismic retrofitting; (c) Contractors and skilled artisans knowledgeable in this are scarce; (d) People at large have no knowledge of the option of retrofitting; and (e) Information on retrofitting is hard to find. As a result, the use of retrofitting as a tool for managing the earthquake risk is fraught with too many obstacles, putting it beyond the reach of an ordinary person. In India, it would not be an exaggeration to say that over 80% buildings that consist of non-engineered masonry are vulnerable against the hazard of future earthquake. These cover a broad range of buildings starting from small mud houses in remote villages all the way to the moderately large infrastructure buildings in cities. With the country witnessing a large number of deaths and incurring huge losses every year resulting from disasters, it is important that the vulnerability of these non-engineered masonry structures is reduced through retrofitting.

Fortunately, a substantial amount of pioneering work has been done in different parts of the country on seismic retrofitting of 'non--engineered masonry' buildings, although by a few individuals. This includes (a) development of regional technical guidelines in a number of regions, (b) making of public awareness materials in the regional languages, and (c) most importantly, the actual execution of retrofitting of local variants of masonry structures coupled with some artisan training on retrofitting. Since each region poses significantly different context, such an effort required each approach to evolve the solutions to tackle the problems on hand peculiar to the area. This involved different building technologies, different materials, difficulties of access, unreliability of electric power, and unavailability of basic as well as special materials needed for retrofitting. The retrofitting work carried out in various regions, although on a small scale, offers a number of lessons that could be valuable for further development of retrofitting as well as for its promotion as the most attractive option for reducing vulnerability.

Four case studies have been taken, which are: (a) a house in a village in Latur region, (b) a road and building department office-cum-storage building in a small Gujarat town, (c) a small school in the mountainous border region of Kashmir, (d) a large three-storey school of Delhi Municipal Corporation.

From the experience of the retrofitting projects undertaken at these and other sites, the following major lessons in regard to the promotion of retrofitting as the principal option for vulnerability reduction emerged:

- The Government policy for managing disaster risk must place top priority on vulnerability reduction of existing non-engineered buildings.
- Awareness creation in the community at large about the possible dangers of a future disaster and the significance of retrofitting is a prerequisite for the promotion of retrofitting.
- Simple booklets and brochures on the subject must be made easily available in local language.
- Government engineers must receive rigorous onsite training in the retrofitting of non-engineered buildings to enable the respective agency to take up retrofitting projects.
- Retrofitting skills must become easily available in the market through the hands-on training programmes for masons.
- Public agencies owning buildings must be made aware of the need for retrofitting these buildings to help them assign right priority to retrofitting.
- Special materials required for retrofitting must be available easily. For the most common building systems, the retrofitting items must be standardized with their specifications, and SOR must be developed and recognized.
- Documentation system also needs to be standardized so that all engineers use the same language of communication.
- Engineering community needs to become proactive in this direction just like in many of the Western countries.

Rescue Operation after UK Train Accident

On 31 January, 1995, the two-car 16:23 h Carlisle-to-Leeds train service was about 2 hours out of Carlisle when it was turned back because of flooding on the track ahead. On its return journey, the train became derailed after hitting a landslide on the track caused by torrential rain. It came to rest across both the 'up' and 'down' lines of a remote section of track on an embankment near the summit of Ais Gill, a hill on the county border between Cumbria and West Yorkshire. At approximately 18:55h, a second two-car Carlisle-to-Leeds train travelling towards Leeds collided at high speed with the derailed train.

The disaster elicited large-scale operations by three emergency services: the Cumbrian Fire Brigade, the Cumbrian Ambulance Service, and the British Transport Police (BTP). Large-scale operations were also mounted by the owners of the track, Railtrack, and by the train operating company, Regional Railways North-East, although these are not reported in detail here. Other responders included the local Cumbrian Police, three local doctors, local mountain rescue teams and the Health and Safety Executive. Two hospitals, in Carlisle and Lancaster, were placed on standby.

All responders had difficulty in locating the accident. At 19:20 h, six fire-fighters from Kirkby Stephen were the first rescuers to reach the site. Following this, resources of the incident organization continued to arrive over the following 4 hours. More fire brigade vehicles arrived during the hour after 19:20 h from Kendal and Sedbergh, and more senior officers attended from Penrith, Barrow-in-Furness and Cockermouth. The first ambulance crew, comprising one paramedic and one ambulance technician from Brough, arrived at 19:44 h and other crews started to arrive aft.er 20:00 h from Sedbergh, Kendal, Brough, and one from the neighbouring authority of West Yorkshire. The first contingent of BTP officers reached the site by car from Carlisle at about 21:40 h, with others arriving later from Lancaster, followed by more senior officers from Preston and Manchester. Special units also arrived later for crime scene investigation and to search the area for evidence and people. Prior to this, a local police sergeant and inspector attended the incident.

The location of the collision was accessible from the road, which was several hundred metres away down a hillside. All units arriving at the scene had to leave their vehicles at the road access point and from there climb by foot up the muddy hillside to the crash point. The response was made difficult by the remoteness and inaccessibility of the location, and by the darkness, cold and torrential rain. However, most of the initial tasks confronting the incident organization were relatively straightforward once the situation had been established. There was no fire in the crashed trains, and fire risks were quickly reduced to an acceptable level. Dangers from the landslide and the instability of the train wreckage, to both casualties and rescue workers, were also quickly established as being acceptable by the fire brigade. Investigation of the accident did not present a difficult challenge as the witnesses could not leave the crash point for an extended period. The conductor of the first train had been killed in the collision, and immediate medical care was administered as far as possible to the other 27 passengers and crew who were left in various states of injury; all needed hospitalization, for examination at least.

Disaster management system at Ais Gill: This structure is consistent with the UK's disaster management scheme. Each agency had a remote communication centre located at Carlisle for the ambulance service and BTP, and at Cocker mouth for the fire brigade. All intra-agency communications between individuals at different locations passed via their communications centre. A number of other communication centres such those of the local police and the railway companies were also involved. For example, Railtrack and the train company used centres at Crewe, Carlisle and York during the incident.

Problem of Inter-agency Co-ordination in Disaster Management

A recurring problem in the management of response to natural and technological disasters, such as extensive bush fires and major transport accidents, is the lack of co-ordination between the various rescue agencies involved. These agencies include not only the emergency services (e.g. police, fire and ambulance), but also local and national government bodies, private sector organizations and volunteer groups.

Each disaster gives rise to the formation of what can be called an *incident organization;* that is, a temporary configuration of otherwise disparate resources drawn from many agencies. Within the incident organization, those distributed people, technologies and procedures concerned with directing resources can be identified collectively as the *disaster management system.* The problem of inter-agency co-ordination lies in the interaction between the structure of this emerging disaster management system and techniques of individual and team decision-making. At this organizational level, considerable effort has gone into the development of special inter-organizational schemes for liaison between agencies. Poor co-ordination in the response to extensive wildfires in the USA in the 1970s, for example, led to the development of the Incident Command System which is now widely used. Similarly, riots and public disturbances in the UK in the 1980s prompted the London Metropolitan Police Force to develop and advocate a unified model of management based on hierarchical levels of 'gold', 'silver' and 'bronze'.

Co-ordination in Decision-making

Inter-agency co-ordination in disaster management is the resolution of interdependencies between activities of the disparate resources of the incident organization. It requires 'dynamic and distributed decision-making'. As the disaster situation unfolds *dynamically,* efforts are made to co-ordinate resources by personnel who are *distributed* across different agencies and locations. These participants in the multi-agency disaster management system can be regarded as a special kind of *team* in the sense that they share common goals, and have distinct roles determined by their agency, rank and location in relation to the disaster. Unlike expert teams, however, such as cockpit flight crews or ship navigators, managers of a disaster situation may not have worked together prior to the incident.

Drawing on research into teamwork, one possible source of difficulty for inter-agency co-ordination might be the absence of an adequate shared mental model (SMM) between participants in the disaster management system. Existence of an SMM would imply a degree of consistency between the various mental models of the disaster held by different individuals. In general, an SMM enables team members to generate similar expectations about a dynamic situation. Questions were applied to two types of SMM that might be held by participants in the disaster management system, referred to here as: One type is task-oriented SMMs, which are models of the situation to be directed encompassing hazards, victims, operational resources and working conditions. The second type is reflexive SMMs, which are models of the disaster management system itself, and are equivalent to Etin and Serfaty's (1999) notion of a 'mutual mental model'.

Index